There Really

Ghosts, Hauntings █████████████████ ██est stories from Dr. H████████████████████ of Parapsychology, █████████████████████ ██is book are accounts █████████████████████ces, cold winds, noises in the night, strange lights and eerie voices. Of the many hundreds of cases that Dr. Holzer has dealt with, *Ghosts, Hauntings and Possessions* focuses on ghosts from the American Revolution to the present— George Washington, Nathan Hale, Henry Clay, Patrick Henry, John La Farge, Alexander Hamilton, Thomas Jefferson, Abraham Lincoln, John and Bobby Kennedy, Elvis Presley ... the list goes on. There are intriguing tales of ancient monks, old men, women and young children. Read about:

- A 37-year-old housewife from Nebraska who was tormented by phantom cars and ghosts at the foot of her bed.
- A psychic who visited the spirit of Thomas Jefferson and learned of the scandals that surrounded his life.
- A seance confrontation with Elvis Presley a year after his death. What was his message from the beyond?
- Ordinary people from all over the country who had premonitions about the murders of John and Robert Kennedy.
- A middle-aged woman who played with the Ouija board and became possessed by the spirit of a former boyfriend.
- Abraham Lincoln's prophetic dream of his own funeral. Does his ghost still roam the White House?

Dr. Holzer also gives insightful views on cases of possession and obsession and a look at just how the dead reveal themselves and communicate through the living.

About the Author

Hans Holzer's interest in parapsychology started early in life—at age three! As a precocious, inquisitive nine year old in Vienna, Austria, he began writing poems and dramas on the subject of ghosts and performed experiments in "raising the dead."

Holzer went on to earn a Ph.D., and today Dr. Holzer is the author of eighty-nine books mainly dealing with psychic subjects and investigations of the paranormal. He has taught parapsychology for many years at the New York Institute of Technology and lectures extensively. Holzer also writes and produces television and feature films, and is a regular guest on television and radio talk shows.

To Write to the Author

We cannot guarantee that every letter written to the author can be answered, but all will be forwarded. Both the author and the publisher appreciate hearing from readers, learning of your enjoyment and benefit from this book. Llewellyn also publishes a bi-monthly news magazine with news and reviews of practical esoteric studies and articles helpful to the student, and some readers' questions and comments to the author may be answered through this magazine's columns if permission to do so is included in the original letter. The author sometimes participates in seminars and workshops, and dates and places are announced in *The Llewellyn New Times*. To write to the author, or to ask a question, write to:

Hans Holzer
c/o THE LLEWELLYN NEW TIMES
P.O. Box 64383-368-X, St. Paul, MN 55164-0383, U.S.A.
Please enclose a self-addressed, stamped envelope for reply, or $1.00
to cover costs.

FATE Presents

Ghosts, Hauntings and Possessions

The Best of Hans Holzer, Book I

Edited by Raymond Buckland

1995
Llewellyn Publications
St. Paul, Minnesota 55164-0383, U.S.A.

FIRST EDITION
Third Printing, 1995

Cover painting by Martin Cannon

Library of Congress Cataloging-in-Publication Data
Holzer, Hans
        [Selections. 1990]
        The best of Hans Holzer / edited by
Raymond Buckland
                p.   cm.—(Fate presents)
        Contents: Book 1. Ghosts, hauntings, and
possessions.
        ISBN 0-87542-367-1 (v. I)
        1. Supernatural. 2. Parapsychology. 3. Occultism.
I. Buckland, Raymond. II. Title. III. Series.
BF 1031.H662   1990
133.8—dc20   90-48679
                                                                CIP

Llewellyn Publications
A Division of Llewellyn Worldwide, Ltd.
P.O. Box 64383, St. Paul, MN 55164-0383

About the FATE Presents Series

Since 1948, FATE magazine has brought to readers around the world true, documented reports of the strange and unusual. For over four decades FATE has reported on such subjects as UFOs and space aliens, Bigfoot, the Loch Ness monster, ESP, psychic powers, divination, ghosts and poltergeists, startling new scientific theories and breakthroughs, real magic, near-death and out-of-body experiences, survival after death, Witches and Witchcraft and many other topics that will even astound your imagination.

FATE has revealed the fakers and the frauds and examined the events and people with powers that defy explanation. If you read it in FATE, the information was certified and factual.

One of the things that makes FATE special is the wide variety of authors who write for it. Some of them have numerous books to their credit and are highly respected in their fields of specialty. Others are plain folks—like you and me—whose lives have crossed over into the world of the paranormal.

Now we are publishing a series of books bearing the FATE name. You hold one such book in your hands. The topic of this book may be one of any of the subjects we've described or a variety of them. It may be a collection of authenticated articles by unknown writers or a book by an author of world-renown.

There is one thing of which you can be assured: the occurrences described in this book are absolutely accurate and took place as noted. Now even more people will be able to marvel at, be shocked by and enjoy *true reports of the strange and unusual.*

Other Books by Hans Holzer

ESP, Witches and UFOs: The Best of Hans Holzer, Book II

The Psychic Side of Dreams

CONTENTS

INTRODUCTION

Since the days of the caveman humankind has been fascinated by thoughts of death and what comes after. The Gravettians (22,000-18,000 B.C.E.) were the first to bury their dead with full clothing; their tools and weapons by their side. They would sprinkle the body with *haematite* (iron peroxide, or red ochre) to give it the appearance of life. They did this almost certainly because they had come to believe in a life after death. Certainly they had found that, in dreams, the living seemed able to again meet with the dead.

We don't know when the first "ghost" was seen but it is probable that its appearance was not frightening to early humans simply because they had come to accept the idea of a life after death, albeit in that strange dreamlike state. But with our modern civilization we have lost so much that is inborn and natural; we have lost the acceptance that was known by early humankind (and is still known, briefly, by young children . . . until they are, unfortunately, programmed out of it).

So what is a ghost? Hans Holzer says it is "the surviving emotional memories of people who are not aware of the transition called death and con-

tinue to function in a thought world as they did at
the time of their passing, or before it." Many times
the spirit of a deceased person does not realize
that, in fact, he or she is dead. They might be
drawn to stay in a particular locale either because
of some traumatic experience they had there or, at
the other end of the scale, because of the great happiness that they knew there. In either case the
need is to cling to that place and those memories,
often to the point of not realizing that they have
died. But it can also be that, although they *do* feel
that they have died, they cannot bring themselves
to *accept* that situation, and so cling to the familiar.

Today there is greater acceptance of the idea
of a life after death than was the case twenty years
ago, or more. Raymond Moody (*Life After Life*) and
Elizabeth Kübler-Ross (*On Death and Dying*) have
done a lot of work on "the death experience," to
show at least the possibility of an afterlife.

In 1901 two Englishwomen, Miss Jourdain
and Miss Moberley, were on a visit to Versailles.
At the Petit Trianon they suddenly found themselves walking through scenes from the eighteenth century! They saw, or so they believed, such
people as Marie Antoinette and members of Louis
XVI's court. Unfortunately what might have been
one of the most grandiose ghost scenes in history is
now held as insignificant because the two ladies
did not bother to put down on paper what they experienced until nine years afterwards. Obviously
human memory can play all kinds of tricks over
that period of time. To have waited just one year

would have been too long.

One man who records, and investigates, ghostly occurrences in a timely and scientific manner, and has made a very fine reputation for himself in the field of "ghost-hunting" and exploration of survival of the death experience, is Dr. Hans Holzer, Professor of Parapsychology. In the 1960s and 1970s, especially, he authored a large number of books dealing with these and peripheral subjects, and appeared on numerous television programs, introducing a vast audience to the world of parapsychology and psychical research. Today he continues to write and speak on the subject.

I have had the pleasure of knowing Dr. Holzer from those early days and therefore was delighted to be asked to edit an anthology of some of his works. I have broken down the chosen excerpts into two volumes: *Ghosts, Hauntings and Possessions (Book I)* and *E.S.P., Witches and UFOs (Book II)*.

The first volume, as might be gathered from the title, deals with apparitions, ghostly appearances, cold winds, noises in the night, strange lights and eerie voices. Of all the many hundreds of cases that Dr. Holzer has dealt with we here look at ghosts from the American Revolution to the present—George Washington, Nathan Hale, Henry Clay, Patrick Henry, John LaFarge, Alexander Hamilton, Thomas Jefferson, Abraham Lincoln, John F. Kennedy and Bobby Kennedy . . . the list goes on. There are ghosts of ancient monks, old men, women and young children and seances to speak with the likes of Elvis Presley. We round out the volume with Dr. Holzer's insightful views on cases of possession and of obsession and a look at just how the dead come to us, and communicate, through the living.

Volume two follows on naturally from the previous volume, dealing with life after death, with telepathy and astral projection, prophetic dreams, healing, paganism and witchcraft, and a good hard look at the probability of "flying saucers."

But first, a proper introduction of Dr. Hans Holzer. Born in Austria, an Aquarian, his interest in ghosts started at a very early age . . . at three years old! In kindergarten, in his native Vienna, he scared his fellow classmates with stories of ghosts to the point where his teacher considered expelling him. From there he went on to enter public school one year ahead of his time (it took a special *ukase* from the Minister of Education, not to mention a large sum of money from his parents, to put him there). As he grew, he developed rapidly to where, by age nine, he was writing poems and "dramas" on the subject of ghosts. By his own admission these stories now "had more terror in them, since I had absorbed a certain amount of mayhem, thanks to the educational motion pictures we were treated to in those days."

On visits to his Uncle Henry, who lived in Bruenn, young Hans assisted in what they termed "raising the spirits"; weird rites taken from his uncle's collection of ancient occult books and performed naively as "experiments." Together they did candleburning rituals, and talked for hours on the possible reality of the other world and spirit communication. At fifteen he became a collector of coins, antiques and—especially—books. Discovery of an old copy of Dr. T. K. Oesterreich's *Occultism In This Modern Age* started him on a more serious approach to ghosts. In school he majored in history and archeology, a background which placed him in good stead for his later career of writer and lecturer.

At age eighteen, in 1938, Hans finally realized his dream of "returning" to America (his father had lived there previously but had gone back to Austria before Hans was born). His first jobs, in New York, were in the world of his expertise at that time—coins and antiques. He rose to become associate editor of a scientific magazine dealing with these but then quit in order to freelance as a writer. In this capacity his old interest in the occult revived.

By 1950 Hans was writing plays and music and was visiting Europe as an accredited foreign correspondent. In London he was covering the theatre when he met Michael Bentine, a comedian appearing at the London Hippodrome (Michael Bentine was one of the original cast members of the BBC's "Goon Show," with Peter Sellers, Spike Milligan, and Harry Secombe), and developed a close friendship with him. They were both born on the same day, both vegetarians, and both had a great interest in the occult. As an indirect result of their lengthy conversations, Hans started work on a television series based on actual hauntings.

Another friend Hans made, in New York, was

the late great psychic Eileen Garrett, long-time President of the Parapsychology Foundation of New York. As he says, "she taught me to be cautious and painstaking, so that the results of my research would not be open to question."

Today Dr. Hans Holzer is the author of eighty-nine books dealing largely with psychic subjects and investigations of the paranormal. He has taught parapsychology for many years at the New York Institute of Technology and lectures extensively. He writes and produces television programs and films and was writer/producer of the NBC series "In Search of . . . " (1976-77), plus a number of television specials. Presently he is developing his own series, "Beyond," plus working on various feature films, and is a regular guest on television and radio talk shows. He holds a Ph.D. and has attended Columbia University, New York, and London College of Applied Science, London, England.

It has been a pleasure for me to renew contact with a man who helped shape the attitude of the "general public," regarding its views of the occult. It is a special pleasure to be part of the instrument that brings some of his writing once more before that public; knowing it will open many new eyes, and start many new feet along the path of healthy inquiry.

—Raymond Buckland

A GREENWICH VILLAGE GHOST
*(Ghost Hunter)**

Back in 1953, when I spent much of my time writing and editing material of a most mundane nature, always, of course, with a weather eye cocked for a good case of haunting, I picked up a copy of *Park East* and found to my amazement some very palatable grist for my psychic mills. "The Ghost Of Tenth Street," by Elizabeth Archer, was a well-documented report of the hauntings on that celebrated Greenwich Village street, where artists make their headquarters, and many buildings date back to the eighteenth century.

Up to 1956, the ancient studio building at 51 West 10th Street was a landmark known to many connoisseurs of old New York, but it was demolished to make way for one of those nondescript, modern apartment buildings that are gradually taking away the charm of Greenwich Village, and give us doubtful comforts in its stead.

Until the very last, reports of an apparition, allegedly the ghost of artist John La Farge, who died in 1910, continued to come in. A few houses

---

* The parenthetical title appearing after each chapter heading indicates the book from which excerpts were taken.

down the street is the Church of the Ascension; the altar painting, "The Ascension," is the work of John La Farge. Actually, the artist did the work on the huge painting at his studio, Number 22, in 51 West 10th Street. He finished it, however, in the church itself, "in place." Having just returned from the Orient, La Farge used a new technique involving the use of several coats of paint, thus making the painting heavier than expected. The painting was hung, but the chassis collapsed; La Farge built a stronger chassis and the painting stayed in place this time. Years went by. Oliver La Farge, the great novelist and grandson of the painter, had spent much of his youth with his celebrated grandfather. One day, while working across the street, he was told the painting had fallen again. Dashing across the street, he found that the painting had indeed fallen, and that his grandfather had died *that very instant!*

The fall of the heavy painting was no trifling matter to La Farge, who was equally well known as an architect as he was a painter. Many buildings in New York for which he drew the plans seventy-five years ago are still standing. But the construction of the chassis of the altar painting may have been faulty. And therein lies the cause of La Farge's ghostly visitations, it would seem. The artists at No. 51 insisted always that La Farge could not find rest until he had corrected his calculations, searching for the original plans of the chassis to find out what was wrong. An obsession to redeem himself as an artist and craftsman, then, would be the underlying cause for the persistence with which La Farge's ghost returned to his old haunts.

The first such return was reported in 1944, when a painter by the name of Feodor Rimsky and his wife lived in No. 22. Late one evening, they returned from the opera. On approaching their studio, they noticed that a light was on and the door open, although they distinctly remembered having *left it shut*. Rimsky walked into the studio, pushed aside the heavy draperies at the entrance to the studio itself, and stopped in amazement. In the middle of the room, a single lamp plainly revealed a stranger behind the large chair in what Rimsky called his library corner; the man wore a tall black hat and a dark, billowing velvet coat. Rimsky quickly told his wife to wait, and rushed across the room to get a closer look at the intruder. But the man *just vanished* as the painter reached the chair.

Later, Rimsky told of his experience to a former owner of the building, who happened to be an amateur historian. He showed Rimsky some pictures of former tenants of his building. In two of them, Rimsky easily recognized his visitor, wearing exactly the same clothes Rimsky had seen him in. Having come from Europe but recently, Rimsky knew nothing of La Farge and had never seen a picture of him. The ball dress worn by the ghost had not been common at the turn of the century, but La Farge was known to affect such strange attire.

Three years later, the Rimskys were entertaining some guests at their studio, including an advertising man named William Weber, who was known to have had psychic experiences in the past. But Weber never wanted to discuss this "special talent" of his, for fear of being ridiculed. As the conversation flowed among Weber, Mrs. Weber, and two other guests, the advertising man's wife noticed her husband's sudden stare at a cabinet on the other side of the room, where paintings were stored. She saw nothing, but Weber asked her in an excited tone of voice—"Do you see that man in the cloak and top hat over there?"

Weber knew nothing of the ghostly tradition of the studio or of John La Farge; no stranger could have gotten by the door without being noticed, and none had been expected at this hour. The studio was locked from the *inside*.

After that, the ghost of John La Farge was heard many times by a variety of tenants at No. 51, opening windows or pushing drapes aside, but not until 1948 was he *seen* again.

Up a flight of stairs from Studio 22, but connected to it—artists like to visit each other— was the studio of illustrator John Alan Maxwell. Connecting stairs and a "secret rest room" used by La Farge had long been walled up in the many structural changes in the old building. Only the window of the walled-up room was still visible from the outside. It was in this area that Rimsky felt that the restless spirit of John La Farge was trapped. As Miss Archer puts it in her narrative, "walled in like the Golem, sleeping through the day and close to the premises for roaming through the night."

After many an unsuccessful search of Rimsky's studio, apparently the ghost started to look in Maxwell's studio. In the spring of 1948, the ghost of La Farge made his initial appearance in the illustrator's studio.

It was a warm night, and Maxwell had gone to bed naked, pulling the covers over himself. Suddenly he awakened. From the amount of light coming in through the skylight, he judged the time to be about one or two in the morning. *He had the uncanny feeling of not being alone in the room.* As his eyes got used to the darkness, he clearly distinguished the figure of a tall woman, bending over his bed, lifting and straightening his sheets several times over. Behind her, there was a man staring at a wooden filing cabinet at the foot of the couch. Then he opened a drawer, looked in it, and closed it again. Getting hold of himself, Maxwell noticed that the woman wore a light red dress of the kind worn in the last century, and the man a white shirt and dark cravat of the same period. It never occured to the illustrator that they were anything but *people*; probably, he thought, models in costume working for one of the artists in the building.

The woman then turned to her companion as if to say something, but did not, and walked off toward the dark room at the other end of the studio. The man then went back to the cabinet and leaned on it, head in hand. By now Maxwell had regained his wits and thought the intruders might be burglars, although he could not figure out how they had entered his place, since he had locked it from the *inside* before going to bed! Making a fist, he struck at the stranger, yelling, "Put your hands up!"

His voice could be heard clearly along the empty corridors. *But his fist went through the man and into the filing cabinet.* Nursing his injured wrist, he realized that his visitors had dissolved into thin air. There was no one in the dark room. The door was still securely locked. The skylight, 150 feet above ground, could not very well have served as an escape route *to anyone human.* By now Maxwell knew that La Farge and his wife had paid him a social call.

Other visitors to No. 51 complained about strange winds and sudden chills when passing La Farge's walled-up room. One night, one of Maxwell's lady visitors returned, shortly after leaving his studio, in great agitation, yelling, "That man! That man!" The inner court of the building was glass-enclosed, so that one could see clearly across to the corridors on the other side of the building. Maxwell and his remaining guests saw nothing there.

But the woman insisted that she saw a strange man under one of the old gaslights in the building; he seemed to lean against the wall of the corridor, dressed in old-fashioned clothes and *possessed of a face so cadaverous and deathmask-like, that it set her ascreaming!*

This was the first time the face of the ghost had been observed clearly by anyone. The sight was enough to make her run back to Maxwell's studio. Nobody could have left without being seen through the glass-enclosed corridors and no one had seen a stranger in the building that evening. As usual, he had vanished into thin air.

So much for Miss Archer's account of the La Farge ghost. My own investigation was sparked by her narrative, and I telephoned her at her Long Island home, inviting her to come along if and when we held a seance at No. 51.

I was then working with a group of parapsychology students meeting at the rooms of the Association for Research and Enlightenment (Cayce Foundation) on West Sixteenth Street. The director of this group was a photo-technician of the *Daily News*, Bernard Axelrod, who was the only one of the group who knew the purpose of the meeting; the others, notably the medium, Mrs. Meyers, knew nothing whatever of our plans.

We met in front of Bigelow's drugstore that cold evening, February 23, 1954, and proceeded to 51 West Tenth Street, where the current occupant of the La Farge studio, an artist named Leon Smith, welcomed us. In addition, there were also present the late *News* columnist, Danton Walker, Henry Belk, the noted playwright Bernays, Marguerite Haymes, and two or three others considered students of psychic phenomena. Unfortunately, Mrs. Belk also brought along her pet chihuahua, which proved to be somewhat of a problem.

All in all, there were fifteen people present in the high-ceilinged, chilly studio. Dim light crept through the tall windows that looked onto the courtyard, and one wished that the fireplace occupying the center of the back wall had been working.

We formed a circle around it, with the medium occupying a comfortable chair directly opposite it, and the sitters filling out the circle on both sides; my own chair was next to the medium's.

The artificial light was dimmed. Mrs. Meyers started to enter the trance state almost immediately and only the loud ticking of the clock in the rear of the room was heard for a while, as her breathing became heavier. At the threshold of passing into trance, the medium sudddenly said, "Someone says very distinctly, *Take another step and I go out this window!* The body of a woman . . . close-fitting hat and a plume . . . close-fitting bodice and a thick skirt . . . lands right on face . . . I see a man, dark curly hair, *hooked nose, an odd, mean face* . . . cleft in chin . . . light tan coat, lighter britches, boots, whip in hand, cruel, mean . . . "

There was silence as she described *what I recognized as the face of La Farge.*

A moment later she continued: "I know the face is not to be looked at anymore. It is horrible. It should have hurt but I didn't remember. Not long. I just want to scream and scream."

The power of the woman who went through the window was strong. "I have a strange feeling," Mrs. Meyers said, "I *have to go out that window* if I go into trance." With a worried look, she turned to me and asked, "If I stand up and start to move, *hold me.*" I nodded assurance and the seance continued. A humming sound came from her lips, gradually assuming human-voice characteristics.

The next personality to manifest itself was apparently a woman in great fear. "They're in the courtyard . . . He is coming . . . they'll find me and whip me again. I'll die first. Let me go. I shouldn't talk so loud. Margaret! Please don't let him come. See the child. My child. Barbara. Oh, the steps, I can't take it. Take Bobby, raise her, I can't take it. He is coming . . . *let me go!* I am free!"

With this, the medium broke out of trance and complained of facial stiffness, as well as pain in the shoulder.

Was the frantic woman someone who had been mistreated by an early inhabitant of No. 22? Was she a runaway slave, many of whom had found refuge in the old houses and alleys of the Village?

I requested of the medium's "control" that the most prominent person connected with the studio be allowed to speak to us. But Albert, the control, assured me that the woman, whom he called Elizabeth, was connected with that man. "He will come only if he is of a mind to. He entered the room a while ago."

I asked Albert to describe this man.

"Sharp features, from what I can see. You are closer to him. Clothes . . . nineties, early 1900s."

After a while, the medium's lips started to move, and a gruff man's voice was heard: *"Get out . . . get out of my house."*

Somewhat taken aback by this greeting, I started to explain to our visitor that we were his friends and here to help him. But he didn't mellow.

"I don't know who you are ... who is every-body here. Don't have friends."

"I am here to help you," I said, and tried to calm the ghost's suspicions. But our visitor was not impressed.

"I want help, but not from you ... *I'll find it!*"

He wouldn't tell us what he was looking for. There were additional requests for us to get out of his house. Finally, the ghost pointed the medium's arm toward the stove and intoned—"I put it there!" A sudden thought inspired me, and I said, lightly—"We found it already."

Rage took hold of the ghost in an instant. "You took it ... you betrayed me ... it is mine ... I was a good man."

I tried in vain to pry his full name from him.

He moaned. "I am sick all over now. Worry, worry, worry. Give it to me."

I promised to return "it," if he would cooper-ate with us.

In a milder tone he said, "I wanted to make it so pretty. *It won't move.*"

I remembered how concerned La Farge had been with his beautiful altar painting, and that it should not fall *again*. I wondered if he knew how much time had passed.

"Who is President of the United States now?" I asked.

Our friend was petulant. "I don't know. I am sick. William McKinley." But then he volun-teered—"I knew him. Met him. In Boston. Last year. Many years ago. Who are you? I don't know any friends. *I am in my house.*"

"What is your full name?"

"Why is that so hard? I know William and I don't know my *own* name."

I have seen this happen before. A disturbed spirit sometimes cannot recall his own name or address.

"Do you know you have passed over?"

"I live here," he said, quietly now. "Times changed. I know I am not what I used to be. *It is there!*"

When I asked what he was looking for, he changed the subject to Bertha, without explaining who Bertha was.

But as he insisted on finding "it," I finally said, "You are welcome to get up and look for it."

"I am bound in this chair and can't move."

"Then tell us where to look for it."

After a moment's hesitation, he spoke. "On the chimney, in back . . . it was over there. I will find it, but I can't move now . . . *I made a mistake* . . . I can't talk like this."

And suddenly he was gone.

As it was getting on to half past ten, the medium was awakened. The conversation among the guests then turned to any feelings they might have had during the seance. Miss Archer was asked about the building.

"It was put up in 1856," she replied, "and is a copy of a similar studio building in Paris."

"Has there ever been any record of a murder committed in this studio?" I asked.

"Yes . . . between 1870 and 1900, *a young girl went through one of these windows.* But I did not mention this in my article, as it *apparently* was unconnected with the La Farge story."

"What about Elizabeth? And Margaret?"

"That was remarkable of the medium," Miss Archer nodded. "You see, Elizabeth was La Farge's wife . . . and Margaret, well, she also fits in with his story."

For the first time, the name La Farge had been mentioned in the presence of the medium. But it meant nothing to her in her conscious state.

Unfortunately, the ghost could not be convinced that his search for the plans was unnecessary, for La Farge's genius as an architect and painter has long since belonged to time.

A few weeks after this seance, I talked to an advertising man named Douglas Baker. To my amazement he, too, had at one time occupied Studio 22. Although aware of the stories surrounding the building, he had scoffed at the idea of a ghost. But one night he was roused from deep sleep by the noise of someone opening and closing drawers. Sitting up in bed, he saw a man in Victorian opera clothes in his room, which was dimly lit by the skylight and windows. Getting out of bed to fence off the intruder, he found himself alone, just as others had before him.

No longer a scoffer, he talked to others in the building, and was able to add one more episode to the La Farge case. It seems a lady was passing No. 51 one bleak afternoon when she noticed an odd-looking gentleman in opera clothes standing in front of the building. For no reason at all, the woman exclaimed, "My, you're a funny-looking man!"

The gentleman in the opera cloak looked at her in rage. "Madam—how dare you!"

And with that, *he went directly through the building—the wall of the building, that is!*

Passers-by revived the lady.

Now there is a modern apartment building at 51 West 10th Street. Is John La Farge still roaming its ugly modern corridors? Last night, I went into the Church of the Ascension, gazed at the marvelous altar painting, and prayed a little that he shouldn't *have to*.

A VISIT
WITH ALEXANDER
HAMILTON'S GHOST

(Ghost Hunter)

There stands at Number 27, Jane Street, in New York's picturesque artists' quarters, Greenwich Village, a mostly wooden house dating back to pre-Revolutionary days. In this house Alexander Hamilton was treated in his final moments. Actually, he died a few houses away, at 80 Jane Street, but No. 27 was the home of John Francis, his doctor, who attended him after the fatal duel with Aaron Burr.

However, the Hamilton house no longer exists, and the wreckers are now after the one of his doctor, now occupied by a writer and artist, Jean Karsavina, who has lived there since 1939.

The facts of Hamilton's untimely passing are well known; D. S. Alexander (in his *Political History of the State of New York*) reports that, because of his political enmity, "Burr seems to have deliberately determined to kill him." A letter written by Hamilton calling Burr "despicable" and "not to be trusted with the reins of government" found its way into the press, and Burr demanded an explanation. Hamilton declined, and on June 11, 1804, at Weehawken, New Jersey, Burr took careful aim and his first shot mortally wounded Hamilton. In the boat back to the city, Hamilton regained consciousness, but knew his end was near. He was taken to Dr. Francis' house and treated, but died within a few days at his own home across the street.

Ever since moving into 27 Jane Street, Miss Karsavina has been aware of footsteps, creaking stairs, and the opening and closing of doors; and even the unexplained flushing of a toilet. On one occasion, she found the toilet chain still swinging, when there was no one around! "I suppose a toilet that flushes *would* be a novelty to someone from the eighteenth century," she is quoted in a brief newspaper account in June of 1957.

She also has seen a blurred "shape," without being able to give details of the apparition; her upstairs tenant, however, reports that one night not so long ago, "a man in eighteenth-century clothes, with his hair in a queue," walked into her room, looked at her and walked out again.

Miss Karsavina turned out to be a well-read and charming lady who had accepted the possibility of living with a ghost under the same roof. Mrs. Meyers and I went to see her in March 1960. The medium had no idea where we were going.

At first, Mrs. Meyers, still in waking condition, noticed a "shadow" of a man, old, with a broad face and bulbous nose; a woman with a black shawl whose name she thought was Deborah, and she thought "someone had a case"; she then described an altar of white lilies, a bridal couple, and a small coffin covered with flowers; then a very old woman in a coffin that was richly adorned, with relatives including a young boy and girl looking into the open coffin. She got the name of Mrs. Patterson, and the girl's as Miss Lucy. In another "impression" of the same premises, Mrs. Meyers described "an empty coffin, people weeping, talking, milling around, *and the American Flag atop the coffin*; in the coffin a man's hat, shoes with silver buckles, gold epaulettes. . . ." She then got close to the man and thought his lungs were filling with liquid and he died with a pain in his side.

Lapsing into semitrance at this point, Mrs. Meyers described a party of men in a small boat on the water, then a man wearing white pants and a blue coat with blood spilled over the pants. "Two boats were involved, and it is dusk," she added.

Switching apparently to another period, Mrs. Meyers felt that "something is going on in the cellar, they try to keep attention from what happens downstairs; there is a woman here, being stopped by two men in uniforms with short jackets and round hats with wide brims, and pistols. There is the sound of shrieking, the woman is pushed back violently, men are marching, someone who had been harbored here has to be given up, an old man in a nightshirt and red socks is being dragged out of the house into the snow."

In still another impression, Mrs. Meyers felt herself drawn up toward the rear of the house where "someone died in childbirth"; in fact, this type of death occurred "several times"; in this house. Police were involved, too, but this event or chain of events is of a later period than the initial impressions, she felt. The name Henry Oliver or Oliver Henry came to her mind.

After her return to full consciousness, Mrs. Meyers remarked that there was a chilly area near the center of the downstairs room. There is; I feel it too. Mrs. Meyers "sees" the figure of a slender man, well-formed, over average height, in white trousers, black boots, dark blue coat and tails, white lace in front; *he is associated with George Washington and Lafayette*, and their faces appear to her, too; she feels Washington may have been in this house. The man she "sees" is a *general*, she can see his epaulettes. The old woman and the children seen earlier are somehow connected with this, too. He died young, and there "was fighting in a boat." Now Mrs. Meyers gets the name "W. Lawrence." She has a warm feeling about the owner of the house; he took in numbers of people, like refugees.

A "General Mills" stored supplies here—shoes, coats, almost like a military post; food is being handed out. The name Bradley is given. Then Mrs. Meyers sees an old man playing a cornet; two men in white trousers are "seen" seated at a long table, bent over papers, with a crystal chandelier above.

After the seance, Miss Karsavina confirmed that the house belonged to Hamilton's physician, and as late as 1825 was owned by a doctor, who happened to be the doctor for the Metropolitan Opera House. The cornet player might have been one of his patients.

In pre-Revolutionary days, the house may have been used as headquarters of an "underground railroad."

GHOSTS OF THE REVOLUTION

(White House Ghosts)

Nathan Hale, as every schoolboy knows, was the American spy hanged by the British. He was captured at Huntington Beach and taken to Brooklyn for trial. How he was captured is a matter of some concern to the people of Huntington, Long Island. The town was originally settled by colonists from Connecticut who were unhappy with the situation in that colony. There were five principal families who accounted for the early settlement of Huntington, and to this day their descendants are the most prominent families in the area. They were the Sammes, the Downings, the Busches, the Pauldings, and the Cooks. During the Revolutionary War, feelings were about equally divided among the town people: some were Revolutionaries and some remained Tories. The consensus of historians is that members of these five prominent families, all of whom were Tories, were responsible for the betrayal of Nathan Hale to the British.

All this was brought to my attention by Mrs. Geraldine P. of Huntington. Mrs. P. grew up in what she considers the oldest house in Huntington, although the Huntington Historical Society claims that theirs is even older. Be that as it may, it was there when the Revolutionary War started. Local legend has it that an act of violence took place on the corner of the street, which was then a crossroads in the middle of a rural area. The house in which Mrs. P. grew up stands on that. Mrs. P. suspects that the capture—or, at any rate, the betrayal—of the Revolutionary agent took place on that crossroads. When she tried to investigate the history of her house, she found little cooperation on the part of the local historical society. It was a conspiracy of silence, according to her, as if some people wanted to cover up a certain situation from the past.

The house had had a "strange depressing effect on all its past residents," according to Mrs. P. Her own father, who studied astrology and white magic for many years, has related an incident that occurred several years ago in the house. He awoke in the middle of the night in the master bedroom because he felt unusually cold. He became aware of "something" rushing about the room in wild, frantic circles. Because of his outlook and training, he spoke up, saying, "Can I help you?" But the rushing about became even more frantic. He then asked what was wrong and what could be done. But no communication was possible. When he saw that he could not communicate with the entity, Mrs. P's father finally said, "If I can't help you, then go away." There was a snapping sound, and the room suddenly became quiet and warm again, and he went back to sleep. There have been no other recorded incidents at the house in question. But Mrs. P. wonders if some guilty entity wants to manifest, not necessarily Nathan Hale, but perhaps someone connected with his betrayal.

At the corner of 43rd Street and Vanderbilt Avenue, Manhattan, one of the busiest and noisiest spots in all of New York City, there is a small commemorative plaque explaining that Nathan Hale, the Revolutionary spy, was executed on that spot by the British. I doubt that too many New Yorkers are aware of this, or can accurately pinpoint the location of the tragedy. It is even less likely that a foreigner would know about it. When I suggested to my good friend Sybil Leek that she accompany me to a psychically important spot for an experiment, she readily agreed. Despite the noises and the heavy traffic, the spot being across from Grand Central Station, Sybil bravely stood with me on the street corner and tried to get some sort of psychic impression.

"I get the impression of food and drink," Sybil said. I pointed out that there were restaurants all over the area, but Sybil shook her head. "No, I was thinking more of a place for food and drink, and I don't mean in the present. It is more like an inn, a transit place, and it has some connection with the river. A meeting place, perhaps, some sort of inn. Of course, it is very difficult in this noise and with all these new buildings here."

"If we took down these buildings, what would we see?"

"I think we would see a field and water. I have a strong feeling that there is a connection with water and with the inn. There are people coming and going—I sense a woman, but I don't think she's important. I am not sure ... unless it would mean foreign. I hear a foreign language. Something like *Verchenen*.* I can't quite get it. It is not German."

"Is there anything you feel about this spot?"

"This spot, yes. I think I want to go back two hundred years at least, it is not very clear, 1769 or 1796. That is the period. The connection with the water puzzles me."

"Do you feel an event of significance here at any time?"

"Yes. It is not strong enough to come through to me completely, but sufficiently drastic to make me feel a little nervous."

"In what way is it drastic?"

"Hurtful, violent. There are several people involved in this violence. Something connected with water, papers connected with water, that is part of the trouble."

Sybil then suggested that we go to the right to see if the impressions might be stronger at some distance. We went around the corner and I stopped. Was the impression any stronger?

"No, the impression is the same. Papers, violence. For a name, I have the impression of the letters P. T. Peter. It would be helpful to come here

---

* Verplanck's Point, on the Hudson River, was a Revolutionary strongpoint at the time.

in the middle of the night, I think. I wish I could understand the connection with water, here in the middle of the city."

"Did someone die here?"

Sybil closed her eyes and thought it over for a moment. "Yes, but the death of this person was important at that time and indeed necessary. But there is more to it than just the death of the person. The disturbance involves lots of other things, lots of other people. In fact, two distinct races were involved, because I sense a lack of understanding. I think that this was a political thing, and the papers were important."

"Can you get anything further on the nature of this violence you feel here?"

"Just a disturbed feeling, an upheaval, a general disturbance. I am sorry I can't get much else. Perhaps if we came here at night, when things are quieter."

I suggested we get some tea in one of the nearby restaurants. Over tea, we discussed our little experiment and Sybil suddenly remembered an odd experience she had had when visiting the Hotel Biltmore before. (The plaque in question is mounted on the wall of the hotel.)

"I receive many invitations to go to this particular area of New York," Sybil explained, "and when I go I always get the feeling of repulsion to the extent where I may be on my way down and get into a telephone booth and call the people involved and say, 'No, I'll meet you somewhere else.' I don't like this particular area we just left; I find it very depressing. I *feel trapped.*"

I am indebted to R. M. Sandwich of Richmond, Virginia, for an intriguing account of an E.S.P. experience he has connected with Patrick Henry. Mr. Sandwich stated that he has had only one E.S.P. experience and that it took place in one of the early estate-homes of Patrick Henry. He admitted that the experience altered his previously dim view of E.S.P. The present owner of the estate has said that Mr. Sandwich has not been the only one to experience strange things in that house.

The estate-home where the incident took place is called Pine Flash and is, at the time of writing, owned by E. E. Verdon, a personal friend of Mr. Sandwich. It is located in Hanover County, about fifteen miles outside of Richmond. The house was given to Patrick Henry by his father-in-law. After Henry had lived in it for a number of years, it burned to the ground and was not rebuilt until fifteen years later. During that time Henry resided in the old cottage, which is directly behind the house, and stayed there until the main house had been rebuilt. This cottage is frequently referred to in the area as the honeymoon cottage of young Patrick Henry. The new house was rebuilt exactly as it had been before the fire. As for the cottage, which is still in excellent condition, it is thought to be the oldest wood frame dwelling in Virginia. It may have been there even before Patrick Henry lived in it.

On the Fourth of July, 1968, the Sandwiches had been invited to try their luck at fishing in a pond on Mr. Verdon's land. Since they would be arriving quite early in the morning, they were told that the oars to the rowboat, which they were to use at the pond, would be found inside the old cottage. They arrived at Pine Flash sometime around six a.m. Mrs. Sandwich started unpacking their fishing gear and food supplies, while Mr. Sandwich decided to inspect the cottage. Although he had been to the place several times before, he had never actually been inside the cottage itself.

Here then is Mr. Sandwich's report.

"I opened the door, walked in, and shut the door tight behind me. Barely a second had passed after I shut the door when a strange feeling sprang over me. It was the kind of feeling you would experience if you were to walk into an extremely cold, damp room. I remember how still everything was, and then I distinctly heard footsteps overhead in the attic. I called out, thinking perhaps there was someone upstairs. No one answered, nothing. At that time I was standing directly in front of an old fireplace. I admit I was scared half to death. The footsteps were louder now and seemed to be coming down the thin staircase toward me. As they passed me, I felt a cold, crisp, odd feeling. I started looking around for something, anything that could have caused all this. It was during this time that I noticed the closed door open very, very slowly. The door stopped when it was half open, almost beckoning me to take my leave, which I did at great speed! As I went through that open door, I felt the same cold mass of air I had experienced before. Standing outside, I watched the door slam itself, almost in my face! My wife was still unpacking the car and claims she neither saw nor heard anything."

Rock Ford, the home of General Edward Hand, is located four miles south of Lancaster, Pennsylvania, and commands a fine view of the Conestoga River. The house is not a restoration but a well-preserved eighteenth-century mansion, with its original floors, railings, shutters, doors, cupboards, panelings, and window glass. Even the original wall painting can be seen. It is a four-story brick mansion in the Georgian style, with the rooms grouped around a center hall in the design popular during the latter part of the eighteenth century. The rooms are furnished with antiquities of the period, thanks to the discovery of an inventory of General Hand's estate which permitted the local historical society to supply authentic articles of daily usage wherever the originals had disappeared from the house.

Perhaps General Edward Hand is not as well known as a hero of the American Revolution as others are, but to the people of the Pennsylvania Dutch country he is an important figure, even though he was of Irish origin rather than German. Trained as a medical doctor at Trinity College, Dublin, he came to America in 1767 with the Eighteenth Royal Irish Regiment of Foote. However, he resigned British service in 1774 and came to Lancaster to practice medicine and surgery. With the fierce love of liberty so many of the Irish possess, Dr. Hand joined the Revolutionaries in July of 1775, becoming a lieutenant colonel in the Pennsylvania Rifle Battalion. He served in the army until 1800, when he was discharged as a major general. Dr. Hand was present at the Battle of Trenton, the Battle of Long Island, the Battle of White Plains, the Battle of Princeton, the campaign against the Iroquois, and the surrender of Cornwallis at Yorktown. He also served on the tribunal which convicted Major John Andre, the British spy, and later became the army's adjutant general. He was highly regarded by George Washington, who visited him in his home toward the end of the war. When peace came, Hand became a member of the Continental Congress and served in the Assembly of Pennsylvania as representative of his area. He moved into Rock Ford when it was completed in 1793 and died there in September 1802.

Today, hostesses from a local historical society serve as guides for the tourists who come to Rock Ford in increasing numbers. Visitors are taken about the lower floor and basement and are told of General Hand's agricultural experiments, his medical studies, and his association with George Washington. But unless you ask specifically, you are not likely to hear about what happened to the house after General Hand died. To begin with, the General's son committed suicide in the house. Before long the family died out, and eventually the house became a museum since no one wanted to live in it for very long. At one time, immigrants were contacted at the docks and offered free housing if they would live in the mansion. None stayed. There was something about the house that was not as it should be, something that made people fear it and leave it just as quickly as they could.

Mrs. Ruth S. lives in upstate New York. In 1967 a friend showed her a brochure concerning Rock Ford, and the house intrigued her. Since she was traveling in that direction, she decided to pay Rock Ford a visit. With her family, she drove up to the house and parked her car in the rear. At that moment she had an eerie feeling that something wasn't right. Mind you, Mrs. S. had not been to the house before, had no knowledge about it nor any indication that anything unusual had occurred in it. The group of visitors was quite small. In addition to herself and her family, there were two young college boys and one other couple. Even though it was a sunny day, Mrs. S. felt icy cold.

"I felt a presence before we entered the house and before we heard the story from the guide," she explained. "If I were a hostess there, I wouldn't stay there alone for two consecutive minutes." Mrs. S. had been to many old houses and restorations before but had never felt as she did at Rock Ford.

Revolutionary figures have a way of hanging on to places they liked in life. Candy Bosselmann of Indiana has had a long history of psychic experiences. She is a budding trance medium and not at all ashamed of her talents. In 1964 she happened to be visiting Ashland, the home of Henry Clay, in Lexington, Kentucky. She had never been to Ashland, so she decided to take a look at it. She and other visitors were shown through the house by an older man, a professional guide, and Candy became somewhat restless listening to his historical ramblings. As the group entered the library and the guide explained the beautiful ash paneling taken from surrounding trees (for which the home is named), she became even more restless. She knew very well that it was the kind of feeling that forewarned her of some sort of psychic event. As she was looking over toward the fireplace, framed by two candelabra, she suddenly saw a very tall, white-haired man in a long black frock coat standing next to it. One elbow rested on the mantel, and his head was in his hand, as if he were pondering something very important.

Miss Bosselmann was not at all emotionally involved with the house. In fact, the guided tour bored her, and she would have preferred to be outside in the stables, since she has a great interest in horses. Her imagination did not conjure up what she saw: she knew in an instant that she was looking at the spirit imprint of Henry Clay.

In 1969 she visited Ashland again, and this time she went into the library deliberately. With her was a friend who wasn't at all psychic. Again, the same restless feeling came over her. But when she was about to go into trance, she decided to get out of the room in a hurry.

It is not surprising that George Washington should be the subject of a number of psychic accounts. Probably the best known (and most frequently misinterpreted) story concerns General Washington's vision which came to him during the encampment at Valley Forge, when the fortunes of war had gone heavily in favor of the British, and the American army, tattered and badly fed, was just about falling to pieces. If there ever was need for divine guidance, it was at Valley Forge. Washington was in the habit of meditating in the woods at times and saying his prayers when he was quite alone. On one of those occasions he returned to his quarters more worried than usual. As he busied himself with his papers, he had the feeling of a presence in the room. Looking up, he saw opposite him a singularly beautiful woman. Since he had given orders not to be disturbed, he couldn't understand how she had gotten into the room. Although he questioned her several times, the visitor would not reply. As he looked at the apparition, for that is what it was, the General became more and more entranced with her, unable to make any move. For a while he thought he was dying, for he imagined that the apparition of such unworldly creatures as he was seeing at that moment must accompany the moment of transition.

Finally, he heard a voice, saying, "Son of the Republic, look and learn." At the same time the visitor extended her arm toward the east, and Washington saw what to him appeared like a white vapor at some distance. As the vapor dissipated, he saw the various countries of the world and the oceans that separated them. He then noticed a dark, shadowy angel standing between Europe and America, taking water out of the ocean and sprinkling it over America with one hand and over Europe with the other. When he did this, a cloud rose from the countries thus sprinkled, and the cloud then moved westward until it enveloped America. Sharp flashes of lightning became visible at intervals in the cloud. At the same time, Washington thought he heard the anguished cries of the American people underneath the cloud. Next, the strange visitor showed him a vision of what America would look like in the future, and he saw villages and towns springing up from one coast to the other until the entire land was covered by them.

"Son of the Republic, the end of the century cometh, look and learn," the visitor said. Again Washington was shown a dark cloud approaching America, and he saw the American people fighting one another. A bright angel then appeared wearing a crown on which was written the word Union. This angel bore the American flag, which he placed between the divided nation, saying, "Remember, you are brethren." At that instant, the inhabitants threw away their weapons and became friends again.

Once more the mysterious voice spoke. "Son of the Republic, look and learn." Now the dark angel put a trumpet to his mouth and sounded three distinct blasts. Then he took water from the ocean and sprinkled it on Europe, Asia, and Africa. As he did so, Washington saw black clouds rise from the countries he had sprinkled. Through the black clouds, Washington could see red lights and hordes of armed men, marching by land and sailing by sea to America, and saw these armies devastate the entire country, burn the villages, towns, and cities, and as he listened to the thundering of the cannon, Washington heard the mysterious voice saying again, "Son of the Republic, look and learn."

Once more the dark angel put the trumpet to his mouth and sounded a long and fearful blast. As he did so, a light as of a thousand suns shone down from above him and pierced the dark cloud which had enveloped America. At the same time the angel wearing the word Union on his head descended from the heavens, followed by legions of white spirits. Together with the inhabitants of America, Washington saw them renew the battle and heard the mysterious voice telling him once again, "Son of the Republic, look and learn."

For the last time, the dark angel dipped water from the ocean and sprinkled it on America; the dark cloud rolled back and left the inhabitants of America victorious. But the vision continued. Once again Washington saw the villages, towns, and cities spring up, and he heard the bright angel exclaim, "While the stars remain and the heavens send down dew upon the earth, so long shall the Union last." With that, the scene faded, and Washington beheld once again the mysterious visitor before him. As if she had guessed his question, the apparition then said:

"Son of the Republic, what you have seen is thus interpreted: Three great perils will come upon the Republic. The most fearful is the third, during which the whole world united shall not prevail against her. Let every child of the Republic learn to live for his God, his land, and his Union." With that, the vision disappeared, and Washington was left pondering over his experience.

One can interpret this story in many ways, of course. If it really occurred, and there are a number of accounts of it in existence which lead me to believe that there is a basis of fact to this, then we are dealing with a case of prophecy on the part of General Washington. It is a moot question whether the third peril has already come upon us, in the shape of World War II, or whether it is yet to befall us. The light that is stronger than many suns may have ominous meaning in this age of nuclear warfare.

Washington himself is said to have appeared to Senator Calhoun of South Carolina at the beginning of the War between the States. At that time, the question of secession had not been fully decided, and Calhoun, one of the most powerful politicians in the government, was not sure whether he could support the withdrawal of his state from the Union. The question lay heavily on his mind when he went to bed one hot night in Charleston, South Carolina. During the night, he thought he awoke to see the apparition of General George Washington standing by his bedside. The General wore his presidential attire and seemed surrounded by a bright outline, as if some powerful source of light shone behind him. On the senator's desk lay the declaration of secession, which he had not yet signed. With Calhoun's and South Carolina's support, the Confederacy would be well on its way, having closed ranks. Earnestly, the spirit of George Washington pleaded with Senator Calhoun not to sign the declaration. He warned him against the impending perils coming to America as a divided nation; he asked him to reconsider his decision and to work for the preservation of the Union. But Calhoun insisted that the South had to go its own way. When the spirit of Washington saw that nothing could sway Senator Calhoun, he warned him that the very act of his signature would be a black spot upon the Constitution of the United States. With that, the vision is said to have vanished.

One can easily explain the experience as a dream, coming as it did at a time when Senator Calhoun was particularly upset over the implications of his actions. On the other hand, there is this to consider: shortly after Calhoun had signed the document taking South Carolina into the Confederacy, a dark spot appeared on his hand, a spot that would not vanish and for which medical authorities had no adequate explanation.

Mrs. Margaret Smith, of Orlando, Florida, has had a long history of psychic experiences. She has personally seen the ghostly monks of Beaulieu, England; she has seen the actual lantern of Joe Baldwin, the famous headless ghost of Wilmington, North Carolina; and she takes her "supernatural" experiences in her stride the way other people feel about their musical talents or hobbies. When she was only a young girl, her grandmother took her to visit the von Steuben house in Hackensack, New Jersey. (General F. W. A. von Steuben was a German supporter of the American Revolution who aided General Washington with volunteers who had come over from Europe because of repressions, hoping to find greater freedom in the New World.) The house was old and dusty, the floorboards were creaking, and there was an eerie atmosphere about it. The house had been turned into a historical museum, and there were hostesses to take visitors through.

While her grandmother was chatting with the guide downstairs, the young girl walked up the stairs by herself. In one of the upstairs parlors she saw a man sitting in a chair in the corner. She assumed he was another guide. When she turned around to ask him a question about the room, he was gone. Since she hadn't heard him leave, that seemed rather odd to her, especially as the floorboards would creak with every step. But being young she didn't pay too much attention to this peculiarity. A moment later, however, he reappeared. As soon as she saw him, she asked the question she had on her mind. This time he did not disappear but answered her in a slow, painstaking voice that seemed to come from far away. When he had satisfied her curiosity about the room, he asked her some questions about herself, and finally asked the one which stuck in her mind for many years afterward—"What is General Washington doing now about the British?"

Margaret was taken aback at this question. She was young, but she knew very well that Washington had been dead for many years. Tactfully, she told him that Harry Truman was now president and that the year was 1951. At this information, the man looked stunned and sat down again in the chair. As Margaret watched him in fascinated horror, he faded away.

A VISIT WITH THE
SPIRITED JEFFERSON
(White House Ghosts)

"This typical pre-Revolutionary tavern was a favorite stopping place for travelers," the official guide to Charlottesville says. "With its colonial furniture and china, its beamed and paneled rooms, it appears much the way it did in the days when Jefferson and Monroe were visitors. Monroe writes of entertaining Lafayette as his guest at dinner here, and General Andrew Jackson, fresh from his victory at New Orleans, stopped over on his way to Washington."

The guide, however, does not mention that the tavern was moved a considerable distance from its original place to a much more accessible location where the tourist trade could benefit from it more. Regardless of this comparatively recent change of position, the tavern is exactly as it was, with everything inside, including its ghosts, intact. At the original site, it was surrounded by trees which framed it and sometimes towered over it. At the new site, facing the road, it looks out into the Virginia countryside almost like a manor house. One walks up to the wooden structure over a number of steps and enters the old tavern to the left or, if one prefers, the pub to the right, which is nowadays a coffee shop. Taverns in the eighteenth and early nineteenth centuries were not simply bars or inns; they were meeting places where people could talk freely, sometimes about political subjects. They were used as headquarters for Revolutionary movements or for invading military forces. Most taverns of any size had ballrooms in which the social functions of the area could be held. Only a few private individuals were wealthy enough to have their own ballrooms built into their manor houses.

What is fortunate about Michie Tavern is the fact that everything is pretty much as it was in the eighteenth century, and whatever restorations have been undertaken are completely authentic. The furniture and cooking utensils, the tools of the innkeeper, the porcelain, the china, the metal objects are all of the period, whether they had been in the house or not. As is customary with historical restorations or preservations, whatever is missing in the house is supplied by painstaking historical research, and objects of the same period and the same area are substituted for those presumably lost during the intervening period.

On my first visit to Charlottesville in 1964, Virginia Cloud had wanted me to visit the tavern, but somehow the schedule did not permit it then. This time the four of us arrived in mid-morning, in order to see the tavern before the tourists came— the luncheon crowd might make an interview with the current manager of the coffee shop difficult. The tavern has three floors and a large number of rooms, so we would need the two hours we had allowed ourselves for the visit. After looking at the downstairs part of the tavern, with its "common" kitchen and the over-long wooden table where two dozen people could be fed, we mounted the stairs to the second floor.

Ingrid kept looking into various rooms, sniffing out the psychic presences, as it were, while I followed close behind. Horace Burr and Virginia Cloud kept a respectable distance, as if trying not to "frighten" the ghosts away. That was all right with me, because I did not want Ingrid to tap the unconscious of either one of these very knowledgeable people. Finally we arrived in the third-floor ballroom of the old tavern. I asked Ingrid what she had felt in the various rooms below. "In the pink room on the second floor I felt an argument or some sort of strife but nothing special in any of the other rooms."

"What about this big ballroom?"

"I can see a lot of people around here. There is a gay atmosphere, and I think important people came here; it is rather exclusive, this room. I think it was used just on special occasions."

By now I had waved Horace and Virginia to come closer, since it had become obvious to me that they wanted very much to hear what Ingrid was saying. Possibly new material might come to light, unknown to both of these historians, in which case they might verify it later on or comment upon it on the spot.

"I'm impressed with an argument over a woman here," Ingrid continued. "It has to do with one of the dignitaries, and it is about one of their wives."

"How does the argument end?"

"I think they just had a quick argument here, about her infidelity."

"Who are the people involved?"

"I think Hamilton. I don't know the woman's name."

"Who is the other man?"

"I think Jefferson was here."

"Try to get as much of the argument as you can."

Ingrid closed her eyes, sat down in a chair generally off limits to visitors, and tried to tune in on the past. "I get the argument as a real embarrassment," she began. "The woman is frail, she has a long dress on with lace at the top part around the neck, her hair is light brown."

"Does she take part in the argument?"

"Yes, she has to side with her husband."

"Describe her husband."

"I can't see his face, but he is dressed in a brocade jacket pulled back with buttons down the front and breeches. It is a very fancy outfit."

"How does it all end?"

"Well, nothing more is said. It is just a terrible embarrassment."

"Is this some sort of special occasion? Are there other people here?"

"Yes, oh, yes. It is like an anniversary or something of that sort. Perhaps a political anniversary of some kind. There is music and dancing and candlelight."

While Ingrid is speaking, in an almost inaudible voice, Horace and Virginia were straining to hear what she was saying but not being very successful at it. At this point Horace waved to me, and I tiptoed over to him. "Ask her to get the period a little closer," he whispered in my ear.

I went back to Ingrid and put the question to her. "I think it was toward the end of the war," she said, "toward the very end of it. For some time now I've had the figure 1781 impressed on my mind."

Since nothing further seemed to be forthcoming from Ingrid at this point, I asked her to relax and come back to the present, so that we could discuss her impressions freely.

"The name Hamilton is impossible in this connection," Horace Burr began. But I was quick to interject that the name Hamilton was fairly common in the late eighteenth and early nineteenth centuries and that Ingrid need not have referred to *the* Alexander Hamilton. "Jefferson was here many times, and he could have been involved in this," Burr continued. "I think I know who the other man might have been. But could we, just for once, try questioning the medium on specific issues?"

Neither Ingrid nor I objected, and Horace proceeded to ask Ingrid to identify the couple she had felt in the ballroom. Ingrid threw her head back for a moment, closed her eyes, and then replied. "The man is very prominent in politics, one of the big three or four at the time, and one of the reasons this is all so embarrassing, from what I get, is that the other man is of much lower caliber. He is not one of the big leaders; he may be an officer or something like that."

While Ingrid was speaking, slowly, as it were, I again felt the strange sense of transportation, of looking back in time, which has been coming to me more and more often recently, always unsought and usually one of fleeting duration. "For what it is worth," I said, "while Ingrid is speaking, I also get a very vague impression that all this has something to do with two sisters. It concerns a rivalry between two sisters."

"The man's outfit," Ingrid continued her narrative, "was sort of gold and white brocade and very fancy. He was the husband. I don't see the other man."

Horace seemed unusually agitated at this. "Tell me, did this couple live in this vicinity or did they come from far away on a special anniversary?"

"They lived in the vicinity and came just for the evening."

"Well, Horace?" I said, getting more and more curious, since he was apparently driving in a specific direction. "What was this all about?"

For once, Horace enjoyed being the center of attraction. "Well, it was a hot and heavy situation, all right. The couple were Mr. and Mrs. John Walker—he was the son of Dr. Walker of Castle Hill. And the man, who wasn't here, was Jefferson himself. Ingrid is right in saying that they lived in the vicinity—Castle Hill is not far away from here."

"But what about the special festivity that brought them all together here?"

Horace wasn't sure what it could have been, but Virginia, in great excitement, broke in here. "It was in this room that the waltz was danced for the first time in America. A young man had come from France dressed in very fancy clothes. The lady he danced with was a closely chaperoned girl from Charlottesville. She was very young, and she danced the waltz with this young man, and everybody in Charlottesville was shocked. The news went around town that the young lady had danced with a man holding her, and that was just terrible at the time. Perhaps that was the occasion. Michie Tavern was a stopover for stagecoaches, and Jefferson and the local people would meet here to get their news. Downstairs was the meeting room, but up there in the ballroom the more special events took place, such as the introduction of the waltz."

I turned to Horace Burr. "How is it that this tavern no longer stands on the original site? I understand it has been moved here for easier tourist access."

"Yes," Horace replied. "The building originally stood near the airport. In fact, the present airport is on part of the old estate that belonged to Colonel John Henry, the father of Patrick Henry. Young Patrick spent part of his boyhood there. Later, Colonel Henry sold the land to the Michies. This house was then their main house. It was on the old highway. In turn, they built themselves an elaborate mansion which is still standing and turned this house into a tavern. All the events we have been discussing took place while this building was on the old site. In 1926 it was moved here.

Originally, I think the ballroom we are standing in now was just the loft of the old Henry house. They raised part of the roof to make it into a ballroom because they had no meeting room in the tavern."

In the attractively furnished coffee shop to the right of the main tavern, Mrs. Juanita Godfrey, the manager, served us steaming hot black coffee and sat down to chat with us. "Had anyone ever complained about unusual noises or other inexplicable manifestations in the tavern?" I asked.

"Some of the employees who work here at night do hear certain sounds they can't account for," Mrs. Godfrey replied. "They will hear something and go and look, and there will be nothing there."

"In what part of the building?"

"All over, even in this area. This is a section of the slave quarters, and it is very old."

Mrs. Godfrey did not seem too keen on psychic experiences, I felt. To the best of her knowledge, no one had any unusual experiences in the tavern. "What about the lady who slept here one night?" I inquired.

"You mean Mrs. Milton—yes, she slept here one night." But Mrs. Godfrey knew nothing of Mrs. Milton's experiences.

However, Virginia had met the lady, who was connected with the historical preservation effort of the community. "One night when Mrs. Milton was out of town," Virginia explained, "I slept in her room. At the time she confessed to me that she had heard footsteps frequently, especially on the stairway down."

"That is the area she slept in, yes," Mrs. Godfrey confirmed. "She slept in the ladies' parlor on the first floor."

"What about yourself, Virginia? Did *you* hear anything?"

"I heard noises, but the wood sometimes behaves very funny. She, however, said they were definitely footsteps. That was in 1961."

What had Ingrid unearthed in the ballroom of Michie Taven? Was it merely the lingering imprint of America's first waltz, scandalous to the early Americans but innocent in the light of today? Or was it something more—an involvement between Mrs. Walker and the illustrious Thomas Jefferson? My image of the great American had always been that of a man above human frailties. But my eyes were to be opened still further on a most intriguing visit to Monticello, Jefferson's home.

"You're welcome to visit Monticello to continue the parapsychological research which you are conducting relative to the personalities of 1776," wrote James A. Bear, Jr., of the Thomas Jefferson Memorial Foundation, and he arranged for us to go to the popular tourist attraction after regular hours, to permit Ingrid the peace and tranquillity necessary to tune in on the very fragile vibrations that might hang on from the past.

Jefferson, along with Benjamin Franklin, has become a popular historical figure these days: a play, a musical, and a film have brought him to life, showing him as the shy, dedicated, intellec-

tual architect of the Declaration of Independence.
Jefferson, the gentle Virginia farmer, the man who
wants to free the slaves but is thwarted in his efforts by other Southerners; Jefferson, the ardent
but bashful lover of his wife; Jefferson, the ideal of
virtue and American patriotism—these are the
images put across by the entertainment media, by
countless books, and by the tourist authorities
which try to entice visitors to come to Charlottesville and visit Jefferson's home, Monticello.

Even the German tourist service plugged itself into the Jefferson boom. "This is like a second
mother country for me," Thomas Jefferson is
quoted as saying while traveling down the Rhine.
"Everything that isn't English in our country
comes from here." Jefferson compared the German
Rhineland to certain portions of Maryland and
Pennsylvania and pointed out that the second
largest ethnic group in America at the time were
Germans. In an article in the German language
weekly *Aufbau*, Jefferson is described as the first
prominent American tourist in the Rhineland. His
visit took place in April 1788. At the time Jefferson
was ambassador to Paris, and the Rhine journey
allowed him to study agriculture, customs, and
conditions on both sides of the Rhine. Unquestionably, Jefferson, along with Washington, Franklin,
and Lincoln represents one of the pillars of the
American edifice.

Virginia Cloud, ever the avid historian of her
area, points out that not only did Jefferson and
John Adams have a close relationship as friends
and political contemporaries but there were cer-

tain uncanny "coincidences" between their lives. For instance, both Jefferson and Adams died within hours of each other, Jefferson in Virginia and Adams in Massachusetts, on July 4, 1826—exactly fifty years to the day they had both signed the Declaration of Independence. Adams's last words were, "But Jefferson still lives." At the time that was no longer true, for Jefferson had died earlier in the day.

Jefferson's imprint is all over Charlottesville. Not only did the talented "Renaissance man" design his own home, Monticello, but he also designed the Rotunda, the focal point of the University of Virginia. Jefferson, Madison, and Monroe were members of the first governing board of the University, which is now famous for its school of medicine—and which, incidentally, is the leading university in the study of parapsychology, since Dr. Ian Stevenson teaches here. On our way to Monticello we decided to visit the old Swan Tavern, which had some important links with Jefferson. The tavern is now used as a private club, but the directors graciously allowed us to come in, even the ladies, who are generally not admitted. Nothing in the appointments reminds one of the old tavern, since the place has been extensively remodeled to suit the requirements of the private club. At first we inspected the downstairs and smiled at several elderly gentlemen who hadn't the slightest idea why we were there. Then we went to the upper story and finally came to rest in a room to the rear of the building. As soon as Ingrid had seated herself in a comfortable chair in a corner, I closed the door and asked her what she felt about this place, of which she had no knowledge.

"I feel that people came here to talk things over in a lighter vein, perhaps over a few drinks."

"Was there anyone in particular who was outstanding among these people?"

"I keep thinking of Jefferson, and I'm seeing big mugs; most of the men have big mugs in front of them."

Considering that Ingrid did not know the past of the building as a tavern, this was pretty evidental. I asked her about Jefferson.

"I think he was the figurehead. This matter concerned him greatly, but I don't think it had anything to do with his own wealth or anything like that."

"At the time when this happened, was there a warlike action in progress?"

"Yes, I think it was on the outskirts of town. I have the feeling that somebody was trying to reach this place and that they were waiting for somebody, and yet they weren't really expecting that person."

Both Horace Burr and Virginia Cloud were visibly excited that Ingrid had put her finger on it, so to speak. Virginia had been championing the cause of the man about whom Ingrid had just spoken. "Virginians are always annoyed to hear about Paul Revere, who was actually an old man with a tired horse that left Revere to walk home," Virginia said, somewhat acidly, "while Jack Jouett did far more—he saved the lives of Thomas Jefferson and his legislators. Yet, outside of Virginia, few have ever heard of him."

"Perhaps Jouett didn't have as good a press agent as Paul Revere had in Longfellow, as you always say, Virginia," Burr commented. I asked Virginia to sum up the incident that Ingrid had touched on psychically.

"Jack Jouett was a native of Albermarle County and was of French Huguenot origin. His father, Captain John Jouette, owned this tavern."

"We think there is a chance that he also owned the Cuckoo Tavern in Louisa, forty miles from here," Burr interjected.

"Jouett had a son named Jack who stood six feet, four inches and weighed over two hundred pounds. He was an expert rider and one of those citizens who signed the oath of intelligence to the Commonwealth of Virginia in 1779.

"It was June 3, 1781, and the government had fled to Charlottesville from the advancing British troops. Most of Virginia was in British hands, and General Cornwallis very much wanted to capture the leaders of the Revolution, especially Thomas Jefferson, who had authored the Declaration of Independence, and Patrick Henry, whose motto, 'Give me liberty or give me death,' had so much contributed to the success of the Revolution. In charge of 250 cavalrymen was Sir Banastre Tarleton. His mission was to get to Charlottesville as quickly as possible to capture the leaders of the uprising. Tarleton was determined to cover the seventy miles' distance between Cornwallis's headquarters and Charlottesville in a single twenty-four-hour period, in order to surprise the leaders of the American Independence movement.

"In the town of Louisa, forty miles distant from Charlottesville, he and his men stopped into the Cuckoo Tavern for a brief respite. Fate would have it that Jack Jouett was at the tavern at that moment, looking after his father's business. It was a very hot day for June, and the men were thirsty. Despite Tarleton's orders, their tongues loosened, and Jack Jouett was able to overhear their destination. Jack decided to outride them and warn Charlottesville. It was about ten p.m. when he got on his best horse, determined to take short cuts and side roads, while the British would have to stick to the main road. Fortunately, it was a moonlit night; otherwise he might not have made it in the rugged hill country.

"Meanwhile the British were moving ahead too, and around eleven o'clock they came to a halt on a plantation near Louisa. By two a.m. they had resumed their forward march. They paused again a few hours later to seize and burn a train of twelve wagons loaded with arms and clothing for the Continental troops in South Carolina. When dawn broke over Charlottesville, Jouette had left the British far behind. Arriving at Monticello, he dashed up to the front entrance to rouse Jefferson; however, Governor Jefferson, who was an early riser, had seen the rider tear up his driveway and met him at the door. Ever the gentleman, Jefferson offered the exhausted messenger a glass of wine before allowing him to proceed to Charlottesville proper, two miles farther on. There he roused the other members of the government, while Jefferson woke his family. Two hours later, when Tarleton came thundering into Charlottesville, the government of Virginia had vanished."

"That's quite a story, Virginia," I said.

"Of course," Burr added, "Tarleton and his men might have been here even earlier if it hadn't been for the fact that they first stopped at Castle Hill. Dr. and Mrs. Walker entertained them lavishly and served them a sumptuous breakfast. It was not only sumptuous but also delaying, and Dr. Walker played the perfect host to the hilt, showing Tarleton about the place despite the British Commander's impatience, even to measuring Tarleton's orderly on the living-room door jamb. This trooper was the tallest man in the British army and proved to be six feet, nine and one-quarter inches in height. Due to these and other delaying tactics—and there are hints that Mrs. Walker used her not inconsiderable charms as well to delay the visitors—the Walkers made Jack Jouett's ride a complete success. Several members of the legislature who were visiting Dr. Walker at the time were captured, but Jefferson and the bulk of the legislature, which had just begun to convene early in the morning, got away.

"You see, the legislature of Virginia met in this building, and Ingrid was entirely correct with her impressions. The members of the legislature knew, of course, that the British were not far away, but they weren't exactly expecting them here."

After Thomas Jefferson had taken refuge at the house of a certain Mr. Cole, where he was not

likely to be found, Jouett went to his room at his
father's tavern, the very house we were in. He had
well deserved his rest. Among those who were hiding from British arrest was Patrick Henry. He
arrived at a certain farmhouse and identified himself by saying, "I'm Patrick Henry." But the
farmer's wife replied, "Oh, you couldn't be, because
my husband is out there fighting, and Patrick
Henry would be out there too." Henry managed to
convince the farmer's wife that his life depended
on his hiding in her house, and finally she understood. But it was toward the end of the
Revolutionary War and the British knew very well
that they had for all intents and purposes been
beaten. Consequently, shortly afterward,
Cornwallis suggested to the Virginia legislators
that they return to Charlottesville to resume their
offices.

It was time to proceed to Monticello; the afternoon sun was setting, and we would be arriving
just after the last tourists had left. Monticello,
which every schoolboy knows from its representation on the American five-cent piece, is probably
one of the finest examples of American architec-
ture, designed by Jefferson himself, who lies
buried here in the family graveyard. It stands on a
hill looking down into the valley of Charlottesville,
perhaps fifteen minutes from the town proper.
Carefully landscaped grounds surround the
house. Inside, the house is laid out in classical pro-
portions. From the entrance hall with its famous
clock, also designed by Jefferson, one enters a
large, round room, the heart of the house. On both

sides of this central area are rectangular rooms. To the left is a corner room, used as a study and library from where Jefferson, frequently early in the morning before anyone else was up, used to look out on the rolling hills of Virginia. Adjacent to it is a very small bedroom, almost a bunk. Thus, the entire west wing of the building is a self-contained apartment in which Jefferson could be active without interfering with the rest of his family. On the other side of the round central room is a large dining room leading to a terrace which, in turn continues into an open walk with a magnificent view of the hillside. The furniture is Jefferson's own, as are the silver and china, some of it returned to Monticello in recent years by history-conscious citizens of the area who had purchased it in various ways.

The first room we visited was Jefferson's bedroom. Almost in awe herself, Ingrid touched the bedspread of what was once Thomas Jefferson's bed, then his desk and the books he had handled. "I feel his presence here," she said, "and I think he did a lot of his work in this room, a lot of planning and working things out, till the wee hours of the night." I don't think Ingrid knew that Jefferson was in the habit of doing just that, in this particular room.

I motioned Ingrid to sit down in one of Jefferson's chairs and try to capture whatever she might receive from the past. "I can see an awful lot of hard work, sleepless nights and turmoil. Other than that, nothing."

We went into the library next to the study. "I

don't think he spent much time here really, just for reference." On we went to the dining room to the right of the round central room. "I think that was his favorite room, and he loved to meet people here socially." Then she added, "I get the words plum pudding and hot liquor."

"Well," Burr commented, "he loved the lighter things of life. He brought ice cream to America, and he squirted milk directly from the cow into a goblet to make it froth. He had a French palate. He liked what we used to call floating island, a very elaborate dessert."

"I see a lot of people. It is a friendly gathering with glittering glasses and candlelight," Ingrid said. "They are elegant but don't have on overcoats. I see their white silken shirts. I see them laughing and passing things around. Jefferson is at the table with white hair pulled back, leaning over and laughing."

The sun was setting, since it was getting toward half past six now, and we started to walk out the French glass doors onto the terrace. From there an open walk led around a sharp corner to a small building, perhaps twenty or twenty-five yards distant. Built in the small classical American style as Monticello itself, the building contained two fair-sized rooms, on two stories. The walk led to the entrance to the upper story, barricaded by an iron grillwork to keep tourists out. It allowed us to enter the room only partially, but sufficiently for Ingrid to get her bearings. Outside, the temperature sank rapidly as the evening approached. A wind had risen, and so it was pleasant to be inside the protective walls of the little house.

"Horace, where are we now?" I asked.

"We are in the honeymoon cottage where Thomas Jefferson brought his bride and lived at the time when his men were building Monticello. Jefferson and his family lived here at the very beginning, so you might say that whatever impressions there are here would be of the pre-Revolutionary part of Jefferson's life."

I turned to Ingrid and asked for her impressions. "I feel everything is very personal here and light, and I don't feel the tremendous strain in the planning of things I felt in the Monticello building. As I close my eyes, I get a funny feeling about a bouquet of flowers, some very strong and particular exotic flowers. They are either pink or light red and have a funny name, and I have the feeling that a woman involved in this impression is particularly fond of a specific kind of flower. He goes out of his way to get them for her, and I also get the feeling of a liking for a certain kind of chinaware or porcelain. Someone is a collector and wants to buy certain things, being a connoisseur, and wants to have little knick-knacks all over the place. I don't know if any of this makes any sense, but this is how I see it."

"It makes sense indeed," Horace Burr replied. "Jefferson did more to import rare trees and rare flowering shrubs than anyone else around here. In fact, he sent shipments back from France while he stayed there and indicated that they were so rare that if you planted them in one place they might not suceed. So he planted only a third at

Monticello, a third at Verdant Lawn, which is an old estate belonging to a friend of his, and a third somewhere else in Virginia. It was his idea to plant them in three places to see if they would thrive in his Virginia.

"The name Rousseau comes to mind. Did he know anyone by that name?" Ingrid asked.

"Of course, he was much influenced by Rousseau."

"I also get the feeling of a flickering flame, a habit of staying up to all hours of the morning. Oh, and is there any historical record of an argument concerning this habit of his, between his wife and himself and some kind of peacemaking gesture on someone else's part?"

"I am sure there was an argument," Horace said, "but I doubt that there ever was a peacemaking gesture. You see, their marriage was not a blissful one; she was very wealthy and he spent her entire estate, just as he spent Dabney Carr's entire estate and George Short's entire estate. He went through estate after estate, including his own. Dabney Carr was his cousin, and he married Jefferson's sister, Martha. He was very wealthy, but Jefferson gathered up his sister and the children and brought them here after Carr's death. He then took over all the plantations and effects of Mr. Carr.

"Jefferson was a collector of things. He wrote these catalogues of his own collection, and when he died it was the largest collection in America. You are right about the porcelain, because it was terribly sophisticated at that time to be up on porcelain. The clipper trade was bringing in these rarities, and he liked to collect them."

Since Ingrid had scored so nicely up to now, I asked her whether she felt any particular emotional event connected with this little house.

"Well, I think the wife was not living on her level, her standard, and she was unhappy. It wasn't what she was used to. It wasn't grand enough. I think she had doubts about him and his plans."

"In what sense?"

"I think she was dubious about what would happen. She was worried that he was getting too involved, and she didn't like his political affiliations too well."

I turned to Horace for comments. To my surprise, Horace asked me to turn off my tape recorder since the information was of a highly confidential nature. However, he pointed out that the material could be found in *American Heritage*, and that I was free to tell the story in my own words.

Apparently, there had always been a problem between Jefferson and his wife concerning other women. His associations were many and varied. Perhaps the most lasting was with a beautiful young black girl, about the same age as his wife. She was the illegitimate natural child of W. Skelton, a local gentleman, and served as a personal maid to Mrs. Jefferson. Eventually, Jefferson had a number of children by this girl. He even took her to Paris. He would send for her. This went on for a number of years and eventually contributed to the disillusionment of this girl. She died in a little room upstairs, and they took the coffin up there some way, but when they put it together and got her into the coffin, it wouldn't come downstairs. They had to take all the windows out and lower her on a rope. And what was she doing up there in the first place? All this did not contribute to Mrs. Jefferson's happiness. The irony is that, after Jefferson's death, two of his mulatto children were sent to New Orleans and *sold* as prostitutes to pay his debts. There are said to be some descendants of that liaison still alive today, but you won't find any of this in American textbooks.

Gossip and legend intermingle in small towns and in the countryside. This is especially true when important historical figures are involved. So it is said that Jefferson did not die a natural death. Allegedly, he committed suicide by cutting his own throat. Toward the end of Jefferson's life, there was a bitter feud between himself and the Lewis family. Accusations and counteraccusations are said to have gone back and forth. Jefferson is said to have had Merriweather Lewis murdered and, prior to that, to have accused Mr. Lewis of a number of strange things that were not true. But none of these legends and rumors can be proved in terms of judicial procedure; when it comes to patriotic heroes of the American Revolution, the line between truth and fiction is always rather indistinct.

ABRAHAM LINCOLN'S RESTLESS SPIRIT

(White House Ghosts)

All these years after the assassination of President John F. Kennedy we are still not sure of his murderer or murderers, even though the deed was done in the cold glare of a public parade, under the watchful eyes of numerous police and security guards, not to mention admirers in the streets.

While we are still arguing the merits of various theories concerning President Kennedy's assassination we sometimes forget that an earlier crime of a similar nature is equally unresolved. In fact, there are so many startling parallels between the two events that one cannot help but marvel.

One of the people who marveled at them in a particularly impressive way recently is a New York psychiatrist named Stanley Krippner, attached to Maimonides Medical Center, Brooklyn, who has set down his findings in the learned *Journal of Parapsychology*. Among the facts unearthed by Dr. Krippner is the remarkable "death circle" of presidential deaths: Harrison, elected in 1840, died in 1841; Lincoln, elected twenty years later, in 1860, died in 1865; Garfield, elected in 1880, was assassinated in 1881; McKinley, elected in 1900, died by a murderer's hand in 1901; Harding, elected just twenty years after him, died in office in 1923; Roosevelt, reelected in 1940, died in 1945.

Lincoln had many premonitions of being killed. Kennedy's assassination was predicted by Jeane Dixon as early as 1952, and several other seers in 1957 and 1960, not to forget President Kennedy's own expressed feelings of imminent doom.

But far be it from me to suggest that the two Presidents might be personally linked, perhaps through reincarnation, if such could be proved. Their similar fates must be the result of a higher order of which we know as yet very little except that it exists and operates as clearly and deliberately as any other law of nature.

But there is ample reason to reject any notion of Lincoln's rebirth in another body, if anyone were to make such a claim. Mr. Lincoln's *ghost* has been observed in the White House by competent witnesses.

It is natural to assume that in so emotion-laden a building as the White House there might be remnants of people whose lives were very closely tied to the structure. I have defined ghosts as the surviving emotional memories of people who are not aware of the transition called death and continue to function in a thought world as they did at the time of their passing, or before it. In a way, then, they are psychotics unable or unwilling to accept the realities of the nonphysical world into which they properly belong, but which is denied them by their unnatural state of "hanging on" in the denser, physical world of flesh and blood. I am sure we don't know all the unhapppy or disturbed individuals who are bound up with the White House, and some of them may not necessarily be from the distant past, either. But Abigail Adams was seen and identified during the administration of President Taft. Her shade was seen to pass through the doors of the East Room, which was later to play a prominent role in the White House's most famous ghost story.

That Abraham Lincoln would have excellent cause to hang around his former center of activity, even though he died across town, is obvious: he had so much unfinished business of great importance.

Furthermore, Lincoln himself, during his lifetime, had on the record shown an unusual interest in the psychic. The Lincoln family later vehemently denied that seances took placc in thc White House during his administration. Robert Lincoln may have burned some important papers of his father's bearing on these sittings, along with those concerning the political plot to assassinate his father. According to the record, he most certainly destroyed many documents before being halted in this foolish enterprise by a Mr. Young. This happened shortly before Robert Lincoln's death and is attested to by Lincoln authority Emanuel Hertz in *The Hidden Lincoln*.

The spiritualists even go so far as to claim the President as one of their own. This may be extending the facts, but Abraham Lincoln was certainly psychic, and even during his term in the White House his interest in the occult was well known.

The Cleveland Plain Dealer, about to write of Lincoln's interest in this subject, asked the President's permission to do so, or, if he preferred, that he deny the statements made in the article linking him to these activities. Far from denying it, Lincoln replied, "The only falsehood in the statement is that half of it has not been told. The article does not begin to tell the things I have witnessed."

The seances held in the White House may well have started when Lincoln's little boy Willie followed another son, Eddie, into premature death, and Mrs. Lincoln's mind gave way to a state of temporary insanity. Perhaps to soothe her feelings, Lincoln decided to hold seances in the White House. It is not known whether the results were positive or not, but Willie's ghost has also been seen in the White House. During Grant's administration, according to Arthur Krock, a boy whom they recognized as the apparition of little Willie "materialized" before the eyes of some of his household.

The medium Lincoln most frequently used was one Nettie Colburn Maynard, and allegedly the spirit of Daniel Webster communicated with him through her. On that occasion, it is said, he was urged to proclaim the emancipation of the slaves. That proclamation, as everybody knows, became Lincoln's greatest political achievement. What is less known is the fact that it also laid the foundation for later dissension among his Cabinet members and that, as we shall see, it may indirectly have caused his premature death. Before going into this, however, let us make clear that on the whole Lincoln apparently did not need any mediums, for he himself had the gift of clairvoyance, and this talent stayed with him all his life. One of the more remarkable premonitory experiences is reported by Phillip Van Doren Sterm in *The Man Who Killed Lincoln*, and also in most other sources dealing with Lincoln.

It happened in Springfield in 1860, just after Lincoln had been elected. As he was looking at himself in a mirror, he suddenly saw a double image of himself. One, real and life-like, and an etheric double, pale and shadowy. He was convinced that it meant he would get through his first term safely, but would die before the end of the second. Today, psychic researchers would explain Lincoln's mirror experience in less fanciful terms. What the President saw was a brief "out-of-the-body experience," or astral projection; which is not an uncommon psychic experience. It merely means that the bonds between conscious mind and the unconscious are temporarily loosened and that the inner or true self has quickly slipped out. Usually, these experiences take place in the dream state, but there are cases on record where the phenomenon occurs while awake

The President's *interpretation* of the experience is of course another matter; here we have a second phenomenon come into play, that of divination; in his peculiar interpretation of his experience he showed a degree of precognition and future events, unfortunately, proved him to be correct.

This was not, by far, the only recorded dream experienced in Lincoln's life. He put serious stock in dreams and often liked to interpret them. William Herndon, Lincoln's one time law partner and biographer, said of him that he always contended he was doomed to a sad fate, and quotes the President as saying many times, "I am sure I shall meet with some terrible end."

It is interesting to note also that Lincon's fatalism made him often refer to Brutus and Caesar, explaining the events of Caesar's assassination as caused by laws over which neither had any control; years later Lincoln's murderer, John Wilkes Booth, also thought of himself as the new Brutus slaying the American Caesar because destiny had singled him out for the deed!

Certainly the most widely quoted psychic experience of Abraham Lincoln was a strange dream he had a few days before his death. When his strangely thoughtful mien gave Mrs. Lincoln cause to worry, he finally admitted that he had been disturbed by an unusually detailed dream. Urged, over dinner, to confide his dream, he did so in the presence of Ward Hill Lamon, close friend and social secretary as well as a kind of bodyguard. Lamon wrote it down immediately afterward, and it is contained in his biography of Lincoln: "About ten days ago," the President began, "I retired very late. I had been up waiting for important dispatches from the front. I could not have been long in bed when I fell into a slumber, for I was weary. I soon began to dream. There seemed to be a death-like stillness about me. Then I heard subdued sobs, as if a number of people were weeping. I thought I left my bed and wandered downstairs. There the silence was broken by the same pitiful sobbing, but the mourners were invisible. I went from room to room; no living person was in sight, but the same mournful sounds of distress met me as I passed along. It was light in all the rooms; every object was familiar to me; but where were all the people who were grieving as if their hearts would break? I was puzzled and alarmed. What could be the meaning of all this? Determined to find the cause of a state of things so mysterious and so shocking, I kept on until I arrived at the East Room, which I entered.

"There I met with a sickening surprise. Before me was a catafalque, on which rested a corpse wrapped in funeral vestments. Around it were stationed soldiers who were acting as guards; and there was a throng of people, some gazing mournfully upon the corpse, whose face was covered, others weeping pitifully.

"'Who is dead in the White House?' I demanded of one of the soldiers. 'The President,' was his answer; 'he was killed by an assassin!' Then there came a loud burst of grief from the crowd, which awoke me from my dream. I slept no more that night. . . ."

Lincoln always knew he was a marked man, not only because of his own psychic hunches, but objectively, for he kept a sizable envelope in his desk containing all the threatening letters he had received. That envelope was simply marked "Assassination," and the matter did not frighten him.

A man in his position is always in danger, he would argue, although the Civil War and the larger question of what to do with the South after victory had split the country into two factions, making the President's position even more vulnerable. Lincoln therefore did not take his elaborate dream warning seriously, or at any rate, he pretended not to. When his friends remonstrated with him, asking him to take extra precautions, he shrugged off their warnings with the lighthearted remark, "Why, it wasn't me on that catafalque. It was some other fellow!"

But the face of the corpse had been covered in his dream and he really was whistling in the dark.

Had Fate wanted to prevent the tragedy and give him warning to avoid it?

Had an even higher order of things decided that he was to ignore that warning?

Lincoln had often had a certain recurrent dream in which he saw himself on a strange ship, moving with great speed toward an indefinite shore. The dream had always preceded some unusual event. In effect, he had dreamed it precisely in the same way preceding the events at Fort Sumter, the Battles of Bull Run, Antietam, Gettysburg, Stone River, Vicksburg, and Wilmington. Now he had just dreamed it again on the eve of his death. This was the thirteenth of April 1865, and Lincoln spoke of his recurrent dream in unusually optimistic tones. To him it was an indication of impending good news. That news, he felt, would be word from General Sherman that hostilities had ceased. There was a Cabinet meeting scheduled for April 14 and Lincoln hoped the news would come in time for it. It never occurred to him that the important news hinted at by this dream was his own demise that very evening, and that the strange vessel carrying him to a distant shore was Charon's boat ferrying him across the Styx into the non-physical world.

But had he really crossed over?

Rumors of a ghostly President in the White House kept circulating. They were promptly denied by the government, as would be expected. President Theodore Roosevelt, according to Bess Furman in *White House Profile*, often fancied that he felt Lincoln's spirit, and during the administration of Franklin D. Roosevelt, in the 1930s, a girl secretary saw the figure of Abraham Lincoln in his onetime bedroom. The ghost was seated on the bed, pulling on his boots, as if he were in a hurry to go somewhere. This happened in mid-afternoon. Eleanor Roosevelt had often felt Lincoln's presence and freely admitted it.

Now it had been the habit of the administration to put important visitors into what was formerly Lincoln's bedroom. This was not done out of mischief, but merely because the Lincoln room was among the most impressive rooms the White House contained. We have no record of all those who slept there and had eerie experiences, for people, especially politically highly placed people, don't talk about such things as ghosts.

Yet, the late Queen Wilhelmina did mention the constant knockings at her door followed by footsteps—only to find the corridor outside deserted. And Margaret Truman, who also slept in that area of the White House often heard knocking at her bedroom door at 3 a.m. Whenever she checked, there was nobody there. Her father, President Truman, a skeptic, decided that the noises had to be due to "natural" causes, such as the dangerous settling of the floors. He ordered the White House completely rebuilt, and perhaps this was a good thing: It would surely have collapsed soon after, according to the architect, General Edgerton. Thus, if nothing else, the ghostly knockings had led to a survey of the structure and subsequent rebuilding. Or was that the reason for the knocks? Had Lincoln tried to warn the later occupants that the house was about to fall down around their ears?

Not only Lincoln's bedroom, but other old areas of the White House are evidently haunted. There is, first of all, the famous East Room, where the lying in state took place. By a strange quirk of fate, President Kennedy also was placed there after his assassination. Lynda Bird Johnson's room happened to be the room in which Willie Lincoln died, and later on, Truman's mother. It was also the room used by the doctors to perform the autopsy on Abraham Lincoln. It is therefore not too surprising that President Johnson's daughter did not sleep too well in the room. She heard footsteps at night, and the phone would ring and no one would be on the other end. An exasperated White House telephone operator would come on again and again, explaining she did not ring her!

But if Abraham Lincoln's ghost roams the

White House because of unfinished business, it is apparently a ghost free to do other things as well, something the average specter can't do, since it is tied only to the place of its untimely demise.

Mrs. Lincoln lived on for many more years, but ultimately turned senile and died not in her right mind at the home of her sister. Long before she became unbalanced, however, she journeyed to Boston in a continuing search for some proof of her late husband's survival of bodily death. This was in the 1880s, and word had reached her that a certain photographer named William Mumler had been able to obtain the likenesses of dead people on his photographic plates under strictest conditions. She decided to try this man, fully aware that fraud might be attempted if she were recognized. Heavily veiled in mourning clothes, she sat down along with other visitors in Mumler's experimental study. She gave the name of Mrs. Tyndall; all Mumler could see was a widow in heavy veils. Mumler then proceeded to take pictures of all those present in the room. When they were developed, there was one of "Mrs. Tyndall." In back of her appears a semi-solid figure of Abraham Lincoln, with his hands resting upon the shoulders of his widow, and an expression of great compassion on his face. Next to Lincoln was the figure of their son Willie, who had died so young in the White House. Mumler showed his prints to the assembled group, and before Mrs. Lincoln could claim her print, another woman in the group exclaimed, "Why, that looks like President Lincoln!" Then Mrs. Lincoln identified herself for the first time.

There is, by the way, no photograph in existence showing Lincoln with his son in the manner in which they appeared on the psychic photograph. Another photographic likeness of Lincoln was obtained in 1937 in an experiment commemorating the President's one-hundredth birthday. This took place at Cassadaga, Florida, with Horace Hambling as the psychic intermediary, whose mere *presence* would make such a phenomenon possible.

Ralph Pressing, editor of the *Psychic Observer*, was to supply and guard the roll of film to be used, and the exposures were made in dim light inside a seance room. The roll film was then handed to a local photographer for developing, without telling him anything. Imagine the man's surprise when he found a clearly defined portrait of Abraham Lincoln, along with four other, smaller faces, superimposed on the otherwise black negative.

I myself was present at an experiment in San Francisco, when a reputable physician by the name of Andrew von Salza demonstrated his amazing gift of psychic photography, using a Polaroid camera. This was in the fall of 1966, and several other people witnessed the proceedings, which I have reported in my book *Psychic Photography—Threshold of a New Science?*

After I had examined the camera, lens, film, and premises carefully, Dr. von Salza took a number of pictures with the Polaroid camera. On many of them appeared various "extras," or faces of people superimposed in a manner excluding fraud or double exposure completely. The most interesting of these psychic impressions was a picture showing the face of President Lincoln, with President Kennedy next to him!

Had the two men, who had suffered in so many similar ways, found a bond between them in the non-physical world? The amazing picture followed one on which President Kennedy's face appeared alone, accompanied by the word "War" written in white ectoplasm. Was this their way to warn us to "mend our ways"?

Whatever the meaning, I am sure of one thing: the phenomenon itself, the experiment, was genuine and in no way the result of deceit, accident, self-delusion, or hallucination.

THE ILL-FATED
KENNEDY'S
(White House Ghosts)

"When are you going to go down to Dallas and find out about President Kennedy?" the pleasant visitor inquired. He was a schoolteacher who had come to me to seek advice on how to start a course in parapsychology in his part of the country.

The question about President Kennedy was hardly new. I had been asked the same question in various forms ever since the assassination of John F. Kennedy, as if I and my psychic helpers had the duty to use our combined talents to find out what really happened at the School Book Depository in Dallas. I suppose similar conditions prevailed after the death of Abraham Lincoln. People's curiosity had been aroused, and with so many unconfirmed rumors making the rounds the matter of a President's sudden death does become a major topic of conversation and inquiry.

I wasn't there when Lincoln was shot; I was around when President Kennedy was murdered. Thus I am in a fairly good position to trace the public interest with the assassination from the very start.

I assured my visitor that so far I had no plans to go down to Dallas with a medium and find out what "really" happened. I have said so on television many times. When I was reminded that the Abraham Lincoln murder also left some unanswered questions and that I had indeed investigated it and come up with startlingly new results in my book *Window to the Past*, I rejoined that there was one basic difference between the Kennedy death and the assassination of President Lincoln: Lincoln's ghost had been seen repeatedly by reliable witnesses in the White House; so far I have not received any reliable reports of ghostly sightings concerning the late President Kennedy. In my opinion, this meant that the restlessness that caused Lincoln to remain in what used to be his working world has not caused John F. Kennedy to do likewise.

But I am not a hundred per cent sure any longer. Having learned how difficult it is to get information about such matters in Washington, or to gain admission to the White House as anything but a casual tourist—or, of course, on official business—I am also convinced that much may be suppressed or simply disregarded by those to whom experiences have happened simply because we live in a time when psychic phenomena can still embarrass those to whom they occur, especially if they have a position of importance.

But even if John Fitzgerald Kennedy is not walking the corridors of the White House at night, bemoaning his untimely demise or trying to right the many wrongs that have happened in this country since he left us, he is apparently doing something far better. He communicates, under special conditions and with special people. He is far from "dead and gone," if I am to believe those to whom these experiences have come. Naturally, one must sift the fantasy from the real thing— even more so when we are dealing with a famous person. I have done so, and I have looked very closely at the record of people who have reported to me psychic experiences dealing with the Kennedy family. I have eliminated a number of such reports simply because I could not find myself wholly convinced that the one who reported it was entirely balanced. I have also eliminated many other reports, not because I had doubts about the emotional stability of those who had made the reports, but because the reports were far too general and vague to be evidential even in the broadest sense. Material that was unsupported by witnesses, or material that was presented after the fact, was of course disregarded.

With all that in mind, I have come to the conclusion that the Kennedy destiny was something that could not have been avoided whether or not one accepts the old Irish Kennedy curse as factual.

Even the ghostly Kennedys are part and parcel of American life at the present. Why they must pay so high a price in suffering, I cannot guess. But it is true that the Irish forebears of the American Kennedys have also suffered an unusually high percentage of violent deaths over the years, mainly on the male side of the family.

There is, of course, the tradition that way back in the Middle Ages a Kennedy was cursed for having incurred the wrath of some private local enemy. As a result of the curse, he and all his male descendants were to die violently one by one. To dismiss curses as fantasies, or at the very best workable only because of fear symptoms, would not be accurate. I had great doubts about the effectiveness of curses until I came across several cases that allowed of no other explanation. In particular, I refer back to the case of the Wurmbrand curse reported by me in *Ghosts Of the Golden West.* In that case the last male descendant of an illustrious family died under mysterious circumstances quite unexpectedly even while under the care of doctors in a hospital. Thus, if the Kennedy curse is operative, nothing much can be done about it.

Perhaps I should briefly explain the distinction between ghosts and spirits here, since so much of the Kennedy material is of the latter kind rather than the former. Ghosts are generally tied to houses or definite places where their physical bodies died tragically, or at least in a state of unhappiness. They are unable to leave the premises, so to speak, and can only repeat the pattern of their final moments, and are for all practical purposes not fully cognizant of their true state. They can be compared with psychotics in the physical state, and must first be freed from their own self-imposed delusions to be able to answer, if possible through a trance medium, or to leave and become free spirits out in what Dr. Joseph Rhine of Duke University has called "the world of the mind," and which I generally refer to as the non-physical world.

Spirits, on the other hand, are really people,

like you and me, who have left the physical body
but are very much alive in a thinner, etheric body,
with which they are able to function pretty much
the same as they did in the physical body, except
that they are now no longer weighted down by
physical objects, distances, time, and space. The
majority of those who die become free spirits, and
only a tiny fraction are unable to proceed into the
next stage but must remain behind because of
emotional difficulties. Those who have gone on are
not necessarily gone forever, but to the contrary
they are able and frequently anxious to keep a
hand in situations they have left unfinished on the
earth plane. Death by violence or under tragic conditions does not necessarily create a ghost. Some
such conditions may indeed create the ghost syndrome, but many others do not. I should think that
President Kennedy is in the latter group—that is
to say, a free spirit capable of continuing an interest in the world he left behind. Why this is so, I will
show in the next pages.

The R. Lumber Company is a prosperous
firm specializing in the manufacture and whole-
sale of lumber. It is located in Georgia and the
owners, Mr. and Mrs. Bernard R., are respected
citizens in their community. It was in April of 1970
that Mrs. R. contacted me. "I have just finished
reading your book, *Life After Death*, and could not
resist your invitation to share a strange experience with you," she explained, "hoping that you
can give me some opinion regarding its authenticity.

"I have not had an opportunity to discuss what happened with anyone who is in any way psychic or clairvoyant. I have never tried to contact anyone else close to the Kennedys about this, as of course I know they must have received thousands of letters. Many times I feel a little guilty about not ever trying to contact Mrs. Kennedy and the children, if indeed it could have been a genuine last message from the President. It strikes me as odd that we might have received it, or imagined we received it. We were never fans of the Kennedys, and although we were certainly sympathetic to the loss of our President, we were not as emotionally upset as many of our friends were who were ardent admirers.

"I am in no way psychic, nor have I ever had any supernatural experience before. I am a young homemaker and businesswoman, and cannot offer any possible explanation for what happened.

"On Sunday night, November 24, 1963, following John F. Kennedy's assassination, my family and I were at home watching on television the procession going through the Capitol paying their last respects. I was feeling very depressed, especially since that afternoon Oswald had also been killed and I felt we would never know the full story of the assassination. For some strange reason I suddenly thought of the Ouija board, although I have never taken the answers seriously and certainly have never before consulted it about anything of importance. I asked my teen-age daughter to work the board with me, and we went into another room. I had never tried to 'communicate with the dead.' I don't know why I had the courage to ask the questions I did on that night, but somehow, I felt compelled to go on:

Question: Will our country be in danger without Kennedy?

Answer: Strong with, weak without Kennedy, plot—stop.

Question: Will Ruby tell why President was killed?

Answer: Ruby does not know, only Oswald and I know. Sorry.

Question: Will we ever know why Kennedy was killed?

Answer: Underground and Oswald know, Ruby does not know, gangland leader caught in plot.

Question: Who is gangland leader?

Answer: Can't tell now.

Question: Why did Oswald hate President?

Answer: Negroes, civil rights bill.

Question: Have Oswald's and Kennedy's spirits met?

Answer: Yes. No hard feelings in Heaven.

Question: Are you in contact with Kennedy?

Answer: Yes.

Question: Does Kennedy have a message he would send through us?

*Answer:*Yes, yes, yes, tell J. C., and J.J. about this. Thanks, JFK.

Question: Can Kennedy give us some nickname to authenticate this?

Answer: Only nickname 'John John.'

Question: Do you really want us to contact

someone?

Answer: Yes, but wait 'til after my funeral.

Question: How can we be sure Jackie will see our letter?

Answer: Write personal, not sympathy business.

Question: Is there something personal you can tell us to confirm this message?

Answer: Prying public knows all.

Question: Just one nickname you could give us?

Answer: J.J. (John John) likes to swim lots, called 'Daddy's little swimmer boy.' Does that help? JFK.

Question: Anything else?

Answer: J.J. likes to play secret game and bunny.

Question: What was your Navy Serial number?

Answer: 109 P.T. (jg) Skipper–5905. [seemed confused]

Question: Can we contact you again?

Answer: You, JFK, not JFK you.

Question: Give address of your new home.

Answer: Snake Mountain Road.

Question: Will Mrs. Kennedy believe this, does she believe in the supernatural?

Answer: Some—tired—that's all tonight.

"At this point the planchette slid off the bottom of the board marked 'Goodbye' and we attempted no further questions that night.

"The board at all times answered our questions swiftly and deliberately; without hesitation.

It moved so rapidly, in fact, that my daughter and I *could not keep up with the message as it came.* We called out the letters to my eleven-year-old daughter who wrote them down, and we had to unscramble the words after we had received the entire message. We had no intention of trying to communicate *directly* with President Kennedy. I cannot tell you how frightened I was when I asked if there was a message he would send and the message came signed 'JFK.'

"For several days after, I could not believe the message was genuine. I have written Mrs. Kennedy several letters trying to explain what happened, but have never had the courage to mail them.

"None of the answers obtained are sensational, most are things we could have known or guessed. The answers given about 'John John' and 'secret game' and 'bunny' were in a magazine which my children had read and I had not. However, the answer about John John being called 'Daddy's little swimmer boy' is something none of us have ever heard or read. I have researched numerous articles written about the Kennedys during the last two years and have not found any reference to this. I could not persuade my daughter to touch the board again for days. We tried several times in December 1963, but were unsuccessful. One night, just before Christmas, a friend of mine persuaded my daughter to work the board with her. Perhaps the most surprising message came at this time, and it was also the last one we ever received. We are all Protestant and the message was inconsistent with our religious beliefs. When they asked if there was a message from President Kennedy, the planchette spelled out immediately 'Thanks for your prayers while I was in Purgatory, JFK.' "

I have said many times in print and on television that I take a dim view of Ouija boards in general. Most of the material obtained from the use of this instrument merely reflects the unconscious of one or both sitters. Occasionally, however, Ouija boards have been able to tap the psychic levels of a person and come up with the same kind of veridical material a clairvoyant person might come up with. Thus, to dismiss the experiences of Mrs. R. merely because the material was obtained through a Ouija board would not be fair. Taking into account the circumstances, the background of the operators, and their seeming reluctance to seek out such channels of communication, I must discuss ulterior motives such as publicity-seeking reasons or idle curiosity as being the causative factor in the event. On the other hand, having just watched a television program dealing with the demise of President Kennedy, the power of suggestion might have come into play. Had the material obtained through the Ouija board been more specific to a greater extent, perhaps I would not have to hesitate to label this a genuine experience. While there is nothing in the report that indicates fraud—either conscious or unconscious—there is nothing startling in the information given. Surely, if the message had come from Kennedy, or if Kennedy himself had been on the other end of the psychic line, there would have been certain pieces of information that would have been known only to him and that could yet be checked out in a way that was accessible. Surely, Kennedy would have realized how difficult it might have been for an ordinary homemaker to contact his wife. Thus, it seems to me that some other form of proof of identity would have been furnished. This, however, is really only speculation. Despite the sincerity of those reporting the incident, I feel that there is reasonable doubt as to the genuineness of the communication.

By far the majority of communications regarding President Kennedy relate to his death and are in the nature of premonitions, dreams, visions, and other warnings prior to or simultaneous with the event itself. The number of such experiences indicates that the event itself must have been felt ahead of its realization, indicating that some sort of law was in operation that could not be altered, even if President Kennedy could have been warned. As a matter of fact, I am sure that he was given a number of warnings, and that he chose to disregard them. I don't see how he could have done otherwise—both because he was the President and out of a fine sense of destiny that is part and parcel of the Kennedy make-up. Certainly Jeane Dixon was in a position to warn the President several times prior to the assassination. Others, less well connected in Washington, might have written letters that had never got through to the President. Certainly one cannot explain these things away merely by saying a public figure is always in

danger of assassination, or that Kennedy had incurred the wrath of many people in this
country and abroad. This simply doesn't conform
to the facts. Premonitions have frequently been
very precise, indicating in more or less great detail
the manner, time, and nature of the assassination.
If it were merely a matter of vaguely foretelling
the sudden death of the President, then of course
one could say that this comes from a study of the
situation or from a general feeling about the times
in which we live. But this is not so. Many of the
startling predictions couldn't have been made by
anyone, unless they themselves were in on the
planning of the assassination.

Mrs. Rose LaPorta lives in suburban Cleveland, Ohio. Over the years she has developed her
ESP faculties—partially in the dream state and
partially while awake. Some of her premonitory
experiences are so detailed that they cannot be explained on the basis of coincidence, if there is such
a thing, or in any other rational terms. For instance, on May 10, 1963, she dreamed she had
eaten something with glass in it. She could even
feel it in her mouth, so vividly that she began to
spit it out and woke up. On October 4 of that same
year, after she had forgotten the peculiar dream,
she happened to be eating a cookie. There was
some glass in it, and her dream became reality in
every detail. Fortunately, she had told several witnesses of her original dream, so she was able to
prove this to herself on the record.

At her place of work there is a superintendent named Smith, who has offices in another city. There never was any close contact with that man, so it was rather startling to Mrs. LaPorta to hear a voice in her sleep telling her, "Mr. Smith died at home on Monday." Shocked by this message, she discussed it with her coworkers. This was on May 18, 1968. On October 8 of the same year, an announcement was made at the company to the effect that "Mr. Smith died at home on Monday, October 7."

Mrs. LaPorta's ability to tune in on future events reached a national subject on November 17, 1963. She dreamed she was at the White House in Washington on a dark, rainy day. There were beds set up in each of the porticoes. She found herself in the dream, moving from one bed to another, because she wanted to shelter herself from the rain. There was much confusion going on and many men were running around in all directions. They seemed to have guns in their hands and pockets. Finally, Mrs. LaPorta, in the dream, asked someone what was happening, and they told her they were Secret Service men. She was impressed with the terrible confusion and atmosphere of tragedy when she awoke from her dream. That was five days before the assassination happened on November 22, 1963. The dream is somewhat reminiscent of the famed Abraham Lincoln dream, in which he himself saw his own body on the catafalque in the East Room, and asked who was dead in the White House.

Marie Howe is a Maryland housewife, fifty-two years old, and only slightly psychic. The night before the assassination she had a dream in which she saw two brides with the features of men. Upon awakening she spoke of her dream to her husband and children, and interpreted it that someone was going to die very soon. She thought that two persons would die close together. The next day, Kennedy and Oswald turned into the "brides of death" she had seen in her dream.

Bertha Zelkin lives in Los Angeles. The morning of the assassination she suddenly found herself saying, "What would we do if President Kennedy were to die?" That afternoon the event took place.

Marion Confalonieri is a forty-one-year-old housewife, a native of Chicago, has worked as a secretary, and lives with her husband, a draftsman, and two daughters in a comfortable home in California. Over the years she has had many psychic experiences, ranging from *deja vu* feelings to psychic dreams. On Friday, November 22, the assassination took place and Oswald was captured the same day. The following night, Saturday, November 23, Mrs. Confalonieri went to bed exhausted and in tears from all the commotion. Some time during the night she dreamed that she saw a group of men, perhaps a dozen, dressed in suits and some with hats. She seemed to be floating, a little above them, looking down on the scene, and she noticed that they were standing very close in a group. Then she heard a voice say, "Ruby did it." The next morning she gave the dream no particular thought. The name Ruby meant absolutely nothing to her nor, for that matter, to anyone else in the country at that point. It wasn't until she turned her radio on and heard the announcement that Oswald had been shot by a man named Ruby that she realized she had had a preview of things to come several hours before the event itself had taken place.

Another one who tuned in on the future a little ahead of reality was the famed British author, Pendragon, whose real name was L. T. Ackerman. In October 1963, he wrote, "I wouldn't rule out the possibility of attempted assassination or worse if caught off guard." He wrote to President Kennedy urging him that his guard be strengthened, especially when appearing in public.

Dr. Robert G. is a dentist who makes his home in Rhode Island. He has had psychic experiences all his life. At the time when Oswald was caught by the authorities, the doctor's wife wondered out loud what would happen to the man. Without thinking what he was saying, Dr. G. replied, "He will be shot in the police station." The words just popped out of his mouth. There was nothing to indicate even a remote possibility of such a course of action.

He also had a premonition that Robert Kennedy would be shot, but he thought that the Senator would live on with impaired faculties. We know, of course, that Senator Kennedy died. Nevertheless, as most of us will remember, for a time after the announcement of the shooting there was hope that the Senator would indeed continue to live, although with impaired faculties. Not only did the doctors think that might be possible, but announcements were made to that effect. Thus, it is entirely feasible that Dr. G. tuned in not only on the event itself but also on the thoughts and developments that were part of the event.

As yet we know very little about the mechanics of premonitions, and it is entirely possible that some psychics cannot fine-tune their inner instruments beyond a general pickup of future material. This seems to relate to the inability of most mediums to pinpoint exact time in their predictions.

Cecilia Fawn Nichols is a writer who lives in Twenty-nine Palms, California. All her life she has had premonitions that have come true and has accepted the psychic in her life as a perfectly natural element. She had been rooting for John F. Kennedy to be elected President because she felt that his Catholic religion had made him a kind of underdog. When he finally did get the nod, Miss Nichols found herself far from jubilant. As if something foreboding were preying heavily on her mind, she received the news of his election glumly and with a feeling of disaster. At the time she could not explain to herself why, but the thought that the young man who had just been elected was condemned to death entered her mind. "When the unexpected passes through my mind, I know I can expect it," she explained. "I generally do not know just how or when or what. In this case I felt some idiot was going to kill him because of his religion. I expected the assassination much sooner. Possibly because of domestic problems, I wasn't expecting it when it did happen."

On Sunday morning, November 24, she was starting breakfast. Her television set was tuned to Channel 2, and she decided to switch to Channel 7 because that station had been broadcasting the scene directly from Dallas. The announcer was saying that any moment now Oswald would be brought out of jail to be taken away from Dallas. The camera showed the grim faces of the crowd. Miss Nichols took one look at the scene and turned to her mother. "Mama, come in the living room. Oswald is going to be killed in a few minutes, and I don't want to miss seeing it."

There was nothing to indicate such a course of action, of course, but the words just came out of her mouth as if motivated by some outside force. A moment later, the feared event materialized. Along with the gunshot, however, she distinctly heard words said that she was never again to hear on any rerun of the televised action. The words were spoken just as Ruby lifted his arm to shoot. As he began pressing the trigger, the words and the gunshot came close together. Afterwards Miss Nichols listened carefully to many of the reruns but never managed to hear the words again. None of the commentators mentioned them. No account of the killing mentions them. And yet Miss Nichols clearly heard Ruby make a statement even as he was shooting Oswald down.

The fact that she alone heard the words spoken by Ruby bothered Miss Nichols. In 1968 she was with a group of friends discussing the Oswald killing, and again she reported what she had heard that time on television. There was a woman in that group who nodded her head. She too had heard the same words. It came as a great relief to Miss Nichols to know that she was not alone in her perceptions. The words Ruby spoke as he was shooting Oswald were words of anger: "Take this, you son of a bitch!"

This kind of psychic experience is far closer to truthful tuning in on events as they transpire, or just as they are formulating themselves, than some of the more complicated interpretations of events after they have happened.

When it comes to the assassination of Senator Robert Kennedy, the picture is somewhat different. To begin with, very few people thought that Robert Kennedy was in mortal danger, while John F. Kennedy, as President, was always exposed to political danger—as are all Presidents. The Senator did not seem to be in quite so powerful a position. True, he had his enemies, as have all politicians. But the murder by Sirhan Sirhan came as much more of a surprise than the assassination of his brother. It is thus surprising that so much premonitory material exists concerning Robert Kennedy as well. In a way of course, this material is even more evidential because of the lesser likelihood of such an event transpiring.

Mrs. Elaine Jones lives in San Francisco. Her husband is a retired businessman; her brother-in-law headed the publishing firm of Harper & Row; and she is not given to hallucinations. Shortly before the assassination of Robert Kennedy she had a vision of the White House front. At first she saw it as it was and is, and then suddenly the entire front seemed to crumble before her eyes. To her this meant death of someone connected with the White House. A short time later, the assassination of the Senator took place.

Months before the event, famed Washington seeress Jeane Dixon was speaking at the Hotel Ambassador in Los Angeles. She said that Robert Kennedy would be the victim of a "tragedy right here in this hotel." The Senator was assassinated there eight months later.

A young Californian by the name of Lorraine Caswell had a dream the night before the assassination of Senator Kennedy. In her dream she saw the actual assassination as it later happened. The next morning, she reported her nightmare to her roommate, who had served as witness on previous occasions of psychic premonition.

Ellen Roberts works as a secretary, telephonist, and part-time volunteer for political causes she supports. During the campaign of Senator Robert Kennedy she spent some time at

headquarters volunteering her services. Miss
Roberts is a member of the Reverend Zenor's Hollywood Spiritualist Temple. Reverend Zenor,
while in trance, speaks with the voice of Agasha, a
higher teacher, who is also able to foretell events
in the future. On one such occasion, long before the
assassination of John F. Kennedy, Agasha—
through Reverend Zenor—had said, "There will be
not one assassination, but two. He will also be
quite young. Victory will be almost within his
grasp, but he will die just before he assumes the office, if it cannot be prevented."

The night of the murder, Ellen Roberts fell
asleep early. She awakened with a scene of Robert
Kennedy and President Kennedy talking. John F.
Kennedy was putting his arm around his brother's
shoulders and she heard him say, "Well, Bobby,
you made it—the hard way." With a rueful smile
they walked away. Miss Roberts took this to mean
the discomfort that candidate Robert Kennedy
had endured during the campaign—the rock-
throwing, the insults, name-callings, and his
hands had actually become swollen as he was being pulled. Never once did she accept it as
anything more sinister. The following day she realized what her vision had meant.

A curious thing happened to Mrs. Lewis H.
MacKibbel. She and her ten-year-old granddaugh-
ter were watching television the evening of June 4,
1968. Suddenly the little girl jumped up, clasped
her hands to her chest, and in a shocked state announced, "Robert Kennedy has been shot. Shot

down, Mama." Her sisters and mother teased her about it, saying that such an event would have been mentioned on the news if it were true. After a while the subject was dropped. The following morning, June 5, when the family radio was turned on, word of the shooting came. Startled, the family turned to the little girl, who could only nod and say, "Yes I know. I knew it last night."

Mrs. Dawn Chorley lives in central Ohio. A native of England, she spent many years with her husband in South Africa, and has had psychic experiences at various times in her life. During the 1968 election campaign she and her husband, Colin Chorley, had been working for Eugene McCarthy, but when Robert Kennedy won the primary in New Hampshire she was very pleased with that too. The night of the election, she stayed up late. She was very keyed up and thought she would not be able to sleep because of the excitement, but contrary to her expectations she fell immediately into a very deep sleep around midnight. That night she had a curious dream.

"I was standing in the central downstairs room of my house. I was aware of a strange atmosphere around me and felt very lonely. Suddenly I felt a pain in the left side of my head, toward the back. The inside of my mouth started to crumble and blood started gushing out of my mouth. I tried to get to the telephone, but my arms and legs would not respond to my will; everything was disoriented. Somehow I managed to get to the telephone and pick up the receiver. With tremen-

dous difficulty I dialed for the operator, and I could
hear a voice asking whether I needed help, I tried
to say, 'Get a doctor,' but the words came out horri-
bly slurred. Then came the realization I was dying
and I said, 'Oh my God, I am dying,' and sank into
oblivion. I was shouting so loud I awoke my husband, who is a heavy sleeper. Shaking off the
dream, I still felt terribly depressed. My husband,
Colin, noticed the time. Allowing for time changes,
it was the exact minute Robert Kennedy was shot."

Jill Taggart of North Hollywood, California,
had been working with me as a developing medium for several years. By profession a writer and
model, she has been her own worst critic, and in
her reports avoids anything that cannot be sub-
stantiated. On May 14, 1968, she had meant to go
to a rally in honor of Senator Robert Kennedy in
Van Nuys, California. Since the parade was only
three blocks from her house, it was an easy thing
for her to walk over. But early in the evening she
had resolved not to go. To begin with, she was not
fond of the Senator, and she hated large crowds,
but more than anything she had a bad feeling that
something would happen to the Senator while he
was in the car. On the news that evening she heard
that the Senator had been struck in the temple by
a flying object and had fallen to his knees in the
car. The news also reported that he was all right.
Jill, however, felt that the injury was more serious
than announced and that the Senator's reasoning
faculties would be impaired henceforth. "It's possible that it could threaten his life," she reported. "I

know that temples are tricky things." When I spoke to her further, pressing for details, she indicated that she had then felt disaster for Robert Kennedy, but her logical mind refused to enlarge upon the comparatively small injury the candidate had suffered. A short time later, of course, the Senator was dead—not from a stone thrown at him but from a murderer's bullet. Jill Taggart had somehow tuned in on both events simultaneously.

Seventeen-year old Debbie Gaurlay, a high school student who also works at training horses, has had ESP experiences for several years. Two days prior to the assassination of Robert Kennedy she remarked to a friend by the name of Debbie Corso that the Senator would be shot very shortly. At that time there was no logical reason to assume an attempt upon the Senator's life.

John Londren is a machine fitter, twenty-eight years old, who lives with his family in Hartford, Connecticut. Frequently he has had dreams of events that have later transpired. In March 1968 he had a vivid dream in which he saw Senator Robert Kennedy shot while giving his Inaugural Address. Immediately he told his wife and father about the dream, and even wrote a letter to the Senator in April but decided not to send it until after the election. Even the correct names of the assassin and of two people present occurred in his dream. But Mr. Londren dismissed the dream since he knew that Roosevelt Grier and Rafer Johnson were sports figures. He felt they would be out of place in a drama involving the assassination of a political candidate. Nevertheless, those were the two men who actually subdued the killer. In a subsequent dream he saw St. Patrick's Cathedral in New York during Senator Kennedy's funeral. People were running about in a state of panic, and he had the feeling that a bombing or shooting had taken place. So upset was Mr. Londren by his second dream that he asked his father, who had a friend in Washington, to make some inquiries. Eventually the information was given to a Secret Service man who respected extrasensory perception. The New York City bomb squad was called in and the security around the Cathedral was doubled. A man with an unloaded gun was caught fifteen minutes before the President arrived for the funeral at the Cathedral. Mr. Londren's second dream thus proved to be not only evidential but of value in preventing what might have been another crime.

Another amateur prophet is Elaine Morganelli, a Los Angeles housewife. In May 1967 she predicted in writing that President Johnson would be assassinated on June 4, and sent this prediction along with others to her brother, Lewis Olson. What she actually had heard was "President assassination June 4." Well, President Johnson was not assassinated, but on June 5, 1968, Robert Kennedy, a presidential candidate, was shot to death.

It seems clear to me that even the death of Senator Kennedy was part of a predestined master plan, whether we like it or not. Frequently those who are already on the other side of life know what will happen on earth, and if they are not able to prevent it, they are at least ready to help those who are coming across make the transition as painlessly as possible under the circumstances.

To the people of Ireland, the Kennedys can do no wrong. Both Kennedys are great heroes to almost all Irishmen—far more so than they are to Americans. Both these thoughts should be kept in mind as I report still another psychic experience concerning the death of Robert Kennedy.

A fifty-three-year-old secretary by the name of Margaret M. Smith of Chicago, Illinois, was watching the Robert Kennedy funeral on television. As his casket was being carried out of the church to the hearse, she noticed a row of men standing at either side of the casket with their backs to it. They were dressed in gray business suits, very plain, and wore gray hats. These men looked very solemn and kept their eyes cast down. To her they looked liked natives of Ireland. In fact, the suits looked homespun. As the casket went past, one of the men in the line turned his head and looked at the casket. Miss Smith thought that a person in a guard of honor should not do that, for she had taken the man in the gray suit as part of an honor guard. Then it occurred to her that the two lines of men were a little hazy, in a lighter gray. But she took this to be due to the television set, although other figures were quite clear. Later she discussed the funeral with a friend of hers in

another city who had also seen the same broad-
cast. She asked her friend if she knew who the men
in gray had been. Her friend had not seen the men
in gray, nor had any of the others she then asked
about them. Soon it became clear to Mrs. Smith
that she alone had seen the spirit forms of what
she takes to be the Kennedys' Irish ancestors, who
had come to pay their last respects in a fitting
manner.

ELVIS PRESLEY SPEAKS

(Elvis Speaks from the Beyond)

The seance was scheduled for noon, July 13, 1978 and the Drake Hotel in Manhattan was chosen as the site. Dan Schwartz had arranged for a comfortable suite to be ready for us, and in addition to himself, a photographer from the *National Enquirer* was present in the next room. At the appointed hour I arrived at the Hotel Drake, a few minutes before Dorothy Sherry and her mother arrived. I explained to Dorothy that she was not supposed to perform like a trained circus elephant, that there was no punishment if communication proved impossible on this occasion, that another occasion would then be set. Further, I explained to her that the work that she had done alone and with me during the preceding six months had amply proven her ability to establish contact with Elvis Presley, or rather he with her, and that there didn't seem to be any logical reason why this contact should now fail them when so much was at stake in terms of convincing the world of his continued existence in another dimension. Surely, I argued, Elvis would see to it that everything went smoothly. And so he did.

As it turned out, Dee Presley and David
Stanley were somewhat late in arriving, the reason being some additional need for clarification
between themselves and the *National Enquirer*.
This, however, did not concern me, and Dan
Schwartz, ever calm and unruffled, finally
brought the two family members to the suite at the
Hotel Drake. I had met them the night before in order to get the feel of this relationship, and to make
sure that we understood what everybody was expected to do. During that first meeting the
previous day, Dee Presley's literary agent was also
present, a lady of considerable charm whom I had
never met before, or since. It appeared that Mrs.
Presley was working on a book of her own and was
concerned about my clashes of interest. I assured
her that my interests were not so much in a bio-
graphical direction as to anything dealing with
evidence for survival of human personality and the
truth about reincarnation, and that her presence
was being appreciated as an additional piece of
evidence for the authenticity of the communicator,
but that I, as researcher, had already become convinced of that authenticity.

Promptly at noon, on July 13, 1978, we met,
this time without the literary agent, and since
Dorothy seemed ill at ease on the large hotel couch
on which I asked her to sit down, I gave her a light
suggestion, not to induce trance but to calm her. I
sat to her right in an armchair, and opposite me
and to Dorothy's left, Dee Presley took her seat.
Opposite Dorothy, across a table, sat David Stanley, with Dan Schwartz to my right somewhat

further back. The photographer remained in the adjoining room as per instructions. On the table, the *Enquirer* had insisted we place a photograph of the late King of Rock, and a small memorial candle in front of it. It was clear to me from the beginning that Mrs. Presley and David Stanley were polite, but non-commital, in fact, I had the distinct impression that they were more than sceptical about the authenticity of what was to transpire before them. But as the seance continued, their facial expressions changed considerably, and by the time we were finished I had before me two shaken, completely convinced individuals. They had come to scoff, perhaps, but they went home, totally convinced.

Here then is the exact transcript of what transpired in that significant seance confrontation with Elvis Presley on July 13, 1978, nearly a year after he left the physical world.

H.H.: Would you all uncross your legs and relax. If you want to take your shoes off, take your shoes off. Just whatever you want. Be in a quiet, receptive state. You are among friends. We are here to do an experiment— we are opening the door to a man whose contact is desired. We're well aware of the fact that the contact is desired from his side to us and not from us to him. We therefore invite Mr. Presley to make himself known in whatever manner he wishes, to any of us, in any way he sees fit from his standpoint. We offer our services, and

willingness to make the contact.
Several minutes of silence.

H.H.: I therefore call upon Elvis Presley, if he be present, to make himself known in whatever manner he sees fit or suitable to impress Dorothy (and me) whom he has impressed many times before—or any one of us—if that is more to his liking. Our purpose is not to pry, but to make the communication possible in such a way that his intentions are served above all, that his message is carried across to those who care, and, in so doing, that we re-emphasize his identity and continuing existence in a dimension beyond the three-dimensional one.

H.H.: Dorothy, I would like you to be very relaxed and receptive and I would like you to open yourself up to his coming as you have many times before. And though some of the things I may ask you have come before and are therefore known to you from previous visits by him, by Mr. Presley, I would nevertheless sum it up in this manner.

D.S.: He's here now.

H.H.: Has he anything to say?

D.S.: There's a whole pack of them here.

H.H.: Are any of them connected with him?

D.S.: His mother is here.

H.H.: Can you describe his mother?

D.S.: She's short, she's shorter than I am, sad eyes.

H.H.: What color eyes?

D.S.: I don't know.

H.H.: How's she dressed.

D.S.: In a, I don't know what you'd call it, house dress, it's plain, and it's got a belt around the middle. She's very blurry.

H.H.: Does he have anything to say as an opening remark before we go further?

D.S.: He's laughing.

H.H.: Why's he laughing?

D.S.: Giggles. He wants to know if the Colonel has okayed this interview.

H.H.: I'm sure he has or we wouldn't be here.

D.S.: He meant that jokingly.

H.H.: Does he wish to elaborate?

D.S.: No, he's just laughing his fool-head off.

H.H: There are here, apart from you, there are three other people. I hope he's satisfied with their coming.

D.S.: He says he hopes they are satisfied with *his* coming.

H.H.: Well, that would depend to a large degree on him.

D.S.: He's being very ... silly, no, uh, smart and I don't know why.

H.H.: He is aware of course what we're trying to do and why it's important that he's here.

D.S.: Yes.

H.H.: He is aware of the fact that he has arranged all of this and no one else has?

D.S.: Yes.

H.H.: Very well, then it's our intention to do the best we can with what we have on hand. We need his help and cooperation.

D.S.: Yes, sir. Anything I can do. He wants to know, I don't know who he's ... Charley! Where's Charley? Who's Charley?

H.H.: I don't know any Charley.

D.S.: And did his father see a doctor?

H.H.: I don't know the answer, I did pass the message on.

D.S.: I'll have to find out for myself.

H.H.: Is there anything about his father he wishes to tell us?

D.S.: He thinks his father is over-working but that he's becoming almost as well-known as himself.

H.H.: In which way?

D.S.: He has written articles.

H.H.: Well, what about the rest of his family?

D.S.: What about them?

H.H.: Any comment he wishes to make.

D.S.: No.

H.H.: Does he approve or disapprove of anything that's going on.

D.S.: I never saw him here, is there a *cousin here* or am I wrong because his mother said something that I can't quite . . .

H.H.: Why has he brought her?

D.S.: He didn't bring her, she's brought him. Trying to make sure he behaved himself. (laughs)

H.H.: Ask him to talk a little about the conditions under which he now lives.

D.S.: He says, exactly what do you want to know?

H.H.: Ask him, what are your after-life conditions exactly like, from day to day?

D.S.: They go to a school, everybody has a job to do.

H.H.: What is his job?

D.S.: He's watching over me.

H.H.: What is your link from the past?

D.S.: We were married before.

H.H.: How does he feel about reincarnation?

D.S.: He says you can certainly believe it, and this is the whole point to this meeting. He

says if people would just believe it, it
would change the world and mankind
wouldn't be so damn stupid.

H.H.: Anybody present who would be interested
in reincarnation other than you and I?

D.S.: I think it's the lady.

H.H.: Is he pointing at anyone?

D.S.: No, he's pacing up and down.

H.H.: Has he ever discussed reincarnation with
anyone while he was in the physical state?

D.S.: Oh yes, many times.

H.H.: With whom?

D.S.: With everybody, with his father and his
friends. And he says he believed that with
his mind he could do many things. It isn't
as strong as he believed it was then. He
found out he was only a novice. I'm losing
him, I'm sorry. I'm getting too nervous.

H.H.: Relax; there's nothing to be nervous about,
but would you ask him to steady you. I ask
Mr. Presley to please steady her. This is
your instrument, you must help me steady
her.

D.S.: "I told you she's a baby."

H.H.: You're doing fine but you must help us
steady her. Are you in control again? Is he
next to you now?

D.S.: No, he's pacing up and down behind
uh—(points to David Stanley).

H.H.: I would like you to ask Mr. Presley what his connection is to the gentleman, if any?

D.S.: Cousin.

H.H.: Is there anything he wishes to tell us about the gentleman, anything that has occurred between them that we would be very interested in discussing?

D.S.: My grandmother is here now, she's talking.

H.H.: Tell your grandmother to butt out.

D.S.: You don't tell my grandmother to butt out.

H.H.: And kindly stay out, that we have a specific line of inquiry which must be continued; thank you.

D.S.: No, she's still here.

H.H.: Why, what does she have to contribute to this line of inquiry?

D.S.: She says she's here to help if she can.

H.H.: Fine, she's welcome.

D.S.: She says she doesn't butt out for anybody.

H.H.: All right, I'll take it back, but we must stick with the line.

D.S.: She says he's a good boy, leave him alone.

H.H.: Who's a good boy?

D.S.: Elvis.

H.H.: Where's Elvis right now?

D.S.: He's back now.

H.H.: Would you ask him to please come forward again and answer some questions which will be most important to what he's trying to do.

D.S.: He says he's sorry. (laughter)

H.H.: Is he listening to me now?

D.S.: Yes.

H.H.: As far as the gentleman is concerned who is sitting opposite you now, I would like to know if there was anything between them in the way of friendship.

D.S.: Why am I getting a cousin, and then a half-brother?

H.H.: Well, stay with it and don't please question what you're getting.

D.S.: Did someone use a camera on stage during one of the last concerts, someone wrote a poem later, after. He says: 'Hell, they know I'm here.'

H.H.: Who's they?

D.S.: These people.

H.H.: I'd like to know how he feels about this gentleman?

D.S.: Likes him, almost loves him.

H.H.: Have they done anything together, that is important? Ever perform a service for him that was very important at any time?

D.S.: He's standing there laughing. He is standing there laughing his fool-head. He wants it to come across that he wants people to believe that they exist, that they are alive, that they are well, and that they want to communicate with their loved ones. This was the whole purpose, he said.

H.H.: I would like to ask him while we are on the subject—much as I appreciate him being on the other side—there were certain things he liked in this world. Can he talk about some of his favorite possessions?

D.S.: His daughter was his favorite possession.

H.H.: Have you been to his daughter's room with him?

D.S.: No, I've been up in his house.

H.H.: What did you see at the house?

D.S.: I saw his grandmother and some lady who is taking care of his grandmother. She's a very little lady. She's old, she's wrinkled, she's kind of like hunched over.

H.H.: Is she there now?

D.S.: Oh yes.

H.H.: What is in back of the house?

D.S.: It looked like a handball court and it's played with a racquet, and I saw a chain-link fence and there is wrought-iron furniture directly behind in the yard.

H.H.: Were you in Las Vegas with him?

D.S.: Yes.

H.H.: What did the thing look like he took you to?

D.S.: It was a very tall hotel and the parking lot was in the front of the hotel. I kept trying to reject that—here I was, then we went inside, we passed a beautiful lobby, we went off and we made a turn, we were inside a room with a very big stage. I was on that stage. I was also behind it. It's a hallway that has a back elevator where he can go down without having to go through the lobby, without having to go through those people and be mobbed, he was very afraid towards the end of being hurt.

H.H.: Hurt by whom?

D.S.: Fans, crazy people.

H.H.: Was he ever harmed by a fan?

D.S.: In Texas.

H.H.: What happened?

D.S.: He was practically mauled, in the beginning they would tear his clothes all the time, now that he thinks back it was quite funny.

H.H.: Did he think that someone would harm him physically?

D.S.: Yes, he was afraid. There were threats. Threats against his daughter. He wants to know how his daughter is.

H.H.: Was he ever physically threatened or thought he was in danger of his life?

D.S.: Yes, there were phone calls, there was some kind of communication where his father ...

H.H.: A particular situation where his life really was in danger and somebody had to help him?

D.S.: Somebody jumped up on stage. Thought he was being threatened. Went into a total panic.

H.H.: Then what happened?

D.S.: His friends, or so-called friends, they're not his friends anymore. Hell, doesn't even want to discuss them. Quickly pushed, knocked him off the stage.

H.H.: Was there anybody in particular who helped him?

D.S.: Doesn't want to talk about them. They wrote a book that he hopes his father is doing something about—or the Colonel. He thought they were his friends, that they were loyal to him. He's been hurt.

H.H.: By whom?

D.S.: Red, Sonny, David.

H.H.: What about them?

D.S.: There's three of them, they turned against me, they twisted everything and blew it up. Why would they want to talk about me like that?

H.H.: This threat to his life.

D.S.: He wants to get them someday.

H.H.: How does he feel about impersonators?

D.S.: Oh Lordie, he says, ok. He doesn't want them. He says he worked hard, getting where he was and he started from nothing. Why should they use his name? He wants them to stop. He thought you told him that was being taken care of. He's talking to you.

H.H.: I think it is being taken care of.

D.S.: Then why are they still around?

H.H.: These things take time.

D.S.: He says they stink.

H.H.: I'm inclined to agree with him.

D.S.: He says if I ever looked like that I'd never walk on a stage again.

H.H.: Is he interested in psychic healing?

D.S.: Yes. Yes. "I believed I could heal."

H.H.: Did he have the ability?

D.S.: He says he believed he could heal. He says if he had more time.

H.H.: What about his interest in healing?

D.S.:   He was interested in everything.

H.H.:   Did he himself have the power of psychic healing?

D.S.:   He believed he did.

H.H.:   Did he ever discuss it with anybody?

D.S.:   Yes, with his friends, with his associates. He believed there was something with a leg, and he healed it.

H.H.:   Who broke a leg?

D.S.:   Somebody's son, skiing.

H.H.:   You mentioned something about his hands being peculiar in some way.

D.S.:   Bites his nails, he bit his nails or he bites his nails. He still does. The ends of his fingers are extremely rough and the side of his hand is extremely rough.

H.H.:   How is that so?

D.S.:   I don't know, karate?

H.H.:   Did he do that by himself?

D.S.:   No, no he used to work out.

H.H.:   With whom?

D.S.:   Dave, Sonny, you know those guys we talked about before.

H.H.:   What is it that he's complaining about, so we can specify it. I'd like to be sharp about it.

D.S.: "I'm not complaining about anything."

H.H.: But I have the impression he is. Could it be a misunderstanding about certain things?

D.S.: He says there's one thing he couldn't misunderstand.

H.H.: And what is that?

D.S.: It's that book.

H.H.: What is it in that book that he objects to?

D.S.: From the first page to the last.

H.H.: What elements are there, something in it that isn't true?

D.S.: From the first page to the last. They were my friends, they hurt me, by writing that book.

H.H.: Why?

D.S.: They made me sound like I should be in a home, that I was crazy. I was a little crazy, we're all a little crazy. You all know that.

H.H.: Is it that he doesn't like to have books written about him?

D.S.: "This book, they were my friends, don't you understand?"

H.H.: They'd have to be your friends to write about you—they had to know you, a stranger couldn't do it.

D.S.: "They wrote lies, they blew it up, turned on me. They hurt me, they hurt me. I trusted them. I trusted them with my life."

H.H.: Which ones?

D.S.: "Do I have to say it again: Red, Sonny, Dave."

H.H.: Your objection is to some of the things in the book?

D.S.: "Everything in the book."

H.H.: Would you like that someone else would write a book that would rectify matters?

D.S.: "My family. Tell the Colonel he should finally write that book."

H.H.: What about anyone else, what about your family—books are being written already.

D.S.: "Hundreds of them, but they're not me."

H.H.: Did you like jewelry?

D.S.: "Yes."

H.H.: Anything in particular?

D.S.: "There's a diamond cross."

H.H.: What kind of diamond cross?

D.S.: "All diamonds."

H.H.: What's it look like?

D.S.: "Like a cross!"

H.H.: One diamond?

D.S.: "Not one diamond, all diamonds" ... he's talking about something else now, something about Ginger. She was supposed to give it to Lisa.

H.H.:   What kind of jewelry?

D.S.:   A bracelet.

H.H.:   What kind?

D.S.:   She was supposed to give it to Lisa, and she hasn't given it to Lisa.

H.H.:   Is this a message?

D.S.:   Yes, tell her to give it to Lisa. It's a promise. She's keeping it. She's doing all right for herself. She's always in the paper, in the movies. She's doing all right. How's Linda?

H.H.:   What is the bracelet like?

D.S.:   He wants to know how Linda is, he doesn't want to talk about the bracelet now.

H.H.:   Linda, I understand she's well, but can't you go there yourself?

D.S.:   He can't be bothered now, he's busy.

H.H.:   Any other jewelry of his own he wants to talk about now?

D.S.:   He's turning from one mood to the other, he does that often.

H.H.:   I would like him to make a statement because I want to tell the world what his desire is at this time.

D.S.:   He wants people to learn to acknowledge that he (or we) exist because there are many lonely people who want to talk to loved ones and because of total ignorance, utter and complete ignorance—they're fools, they don't learn.

H.H.: I agree with him, this is my message too.

D.S.: They don't learn. Maybe, someday, with your help I can help these people. This is all I want to talk about. This is all I want to discuss. Give my daddy a kiss. (Then, looking directly at David.) A hug and a kiss. Tell him he's all right, and he's happy, and he'll be around.

H.H.: Would you ask him to please talk further to the two people, the lady and the gentleman, and say whatever he wishes. They've come a long way to be here with him.

D.S.: He appreciates that.

H.H.: It would be courteous to talk to them awhile, he may say whatever he wishes.

D.S.: He wants them to give him a hug or a kiss. Tell him he loves him. After all, he's my daddy. He hasn't been well, he wants them to look after him because he can't interfere, he's tired, and because of this ignorance just can't. He says he wants an answer—watch after his father.

H.H.: You want the gentleman to speak. Yes, he will take the message.

D.S.: This lady he talked to on the phone. He's fading again, I'm losing him!

H.H.: I will bring him back.

D.S.:　His mouth is moving, I can see him, but I can't hear him. I'm sorry.

H.H.:　Mr. Presley, please pull your emotions together. It is very important that you stay.

D.S.:　He's pacing. I don't know what's the matter with him. He's impatient.

H.H.:　There are things that you can tell us, that you're debating with yourself.

D.S.:　He has touched this lady, his hand is on her shoulder.

HH.:　Now?

D.S.:　Right now.

H.H.:　Has he touched her before?

D.S.:　No, not since we've gotten here, if that's what you mean.

H.H.:　No, at another time.

D.S.:　He has touched them all before, he has been there and no one noticed. "They don't understand that we're here."

H.H.:　But they can't see him.

D.S.:　They can if they wish.

H.H.:　How?

D.S.:　"Open up, and they will see me, for I will be there."

H.H.:　Is there anything specific that he wants them to do?

D.S.: Just his daddy.

H.H.: What about the lady? She's come a long way to be here. He must have some remarks to address to her, perhaps to the rest of her family.

D.S.: He had a phone call.

H.H.: Who made the call? Explain.

D.S.: He called her.

H.H.: While he was in the flesh?

D.S.: He's shaking his head at me, I'm not getting all of it.

H.H.: Is the phone call important?

D.S.: Yes.

H.H.: What did it deal with?

D.S.: I'm starting to burn again, I'm sorry.

H.H.: He is close to you. Mr. Presley, please, what was the phone call about? Why did you mention it?

D.S.: Hans, I can't hear him.

H.H.: Is he still with you?

D.S.: Yes.

H.H.: He's probably getting excited, if you feel very hot. I would ask that the guides, who are arranging this meeting, stand by, calm the atmosphere, to make communication possible.

D.S.:   God, I'm burning.

H.H.:   Mr. Presley, will you please calm down. You used to take directions, please take directions from me. Now calm down, stand still and we will continue to speak calmly.

D.S.:   He wants to know how come I feel him and no one else can. Does it have to do with our past link?

H.H.:   It had to do with physical ability as well— in the solar plexus area of head and stomach—you know already, you've been taught this in school, but you must be calm or you will be unable to communicate. Now please, Mr. Presley, go behind the lady and leave the instrument for a minute. Do as I tell you.

D.S.:   I'm burning, Hans, I'm burning.

H.H.:   Please let go of the instrument for a second so that we can resume communication.

D.S.:   He says he doesn't understand.

H.H.:   What?

D.S.:   Why is he so hot this time.

H.H.:   Because there has been worry and resistance and the energies being drawn, and you're upset.

D.S.:   He's not moving and I'm burning.

H.H.:   There is nothing to worry about. Give me your hands, please. Calm, relax completely.

D.S.:   He's not moving, he says he's here to protect me.

H.H.:   I know.

D.S.:   And that he's not going to move.

H.H.:   Calm yourself, Mr. Presley, please stay where you are for one second. Disconnect, please. Then reconnect. Disconnect, then reconnect.

D.S.:   What's happening, I don't know what's happening?

H.H.:   He's trying to get you into trance, let go, it's all right. He has something more to say. Please let go of the instrument and go over to the lady for a second.

D.S.:   I've never felt anything like this before. He's very intense.

H.H.:   Because there are people present who mean something to him and he cannot control his emotions. Now break the circuit. Mr. Presley, please go behind the lady opposite me and touch her.

D.S.:   I can't see him.

H.H.:   I want you to stand in back of the lady now and touch her and to calm yourself because we are not going to get any place unless you do. I know it's difficult—you will have to learn to take directions here.

D.S.:   I'm getting a name, something about a psychic named Wright—I can't see him anymore, Hans. He's going in and out.

H.H.: Does he have anything further to tell us. Just calm yourself down for a couple of minutes. Let go completely, relax.

D.S.: I'm starting to burn again.

H.H.: Mr. Presley, will you please stand behind the lady again and you are to relax, let go, and not worry about it anymore.

D.S.: I'm getting hot again, hot.

H.H.: He's emotionally upset, he's trying to push something through.

D.S.: But what?

H.H.: Well, that's what we're here for. To try and find out.

D.S.: I can't see him anymore and I'm burning.

H.H.: Is there something about a cologne or perfume, do you remember it?

D.S.: I remember it but I can't hear him anymore.

H.H.: What is it about the perfume?

D.S.: He had it specially blended.

H.H.: By whom, what was it like?

D.S.: Sweet.

H.H.: The particular scent.

D.S.: I never smelled anything like it before, it's always in my house.

H.H.: Describe it.

D.S.: It's different.

H.H.: What other parts of the house have you been in.

D.S.: The front hall, black and white tiles in the front hall.

H.H.: Did you see him wear any jewelry at any time?

D.S.: No, and he has no suits, just regular trousers or a white shirt.

H.H.: Did he ever tell anybody he trusted them with his life?

D.S.: Yes.

H.H.: Who?

D.S.: I can't hear him but he's here.

H.H.: Let me address him directly. Mr. Presley, do you have anything further to tell us?

D.S.: He says he loves these people, he's not angry he's sorry. Because he's very hot-tempered. He's coming back, because I can see him.

H.H.: He's calming down, I'm sure.

D.S.: This is much stronger than before.

H.H.: Not to worry—Mr. Presley, you understand the need for calm at this particular moment.

D.S.: He says he's trying to help me, he doesn't want to hurt, he doesn't understand what happened. Would you please explain.

H.H.: Well it is his pent-up emotions and some frustration which somehow got out of hand and got into Dorothy because you are holding onto her.

D.S.: I'll always hold onto her, I don't understand.

H.H.: It's a mechanical thing, you are not at fault.

D.S.: "You think I will eventually learn? I'm being taught some things."

H.H.: Yes.

D.S.: Eventually, he says, I'm just a stupid southern boy.

H.H.: You're learning very well, you know already a great deal—not to worry about it.

D.S.: He says I'm learning more each day, I'm trying. He doesn't understand what happened to Dot. He doesn't want to hurt me. Is he hurting me?

H.H.: Not any longer—it's a mechanical thing that happened.

D.S.: He doesn't want to hurt anybody, he never wanted to hurt anybody. And he's starting up again and I'm burning again.

H.H.: No anger please! It would help if he talked about something very unemotional now, would he please talk about psychic healing, how he feels about it.

D.S.: He's pacing again, he's back and forth in front of this couch.

H.H.: Mr. Presley, you have to calm yourself to communicate, there's no other way, and the way to do this is by changing the subject matter.

D.S.: He says I'll walk away if that will help.

H.H.: No, stay, but change the subject.

D.S.: He likes to touch me.

H.H.: Then touch her.

D.S.: He's afraid. He's afraid he's going to hurt me.

H.H.: He can touch you.

D.S.: He always hangs onto me, he says he's my security blanket and that's true. I hang onto him. He says she's a child she has to hold onto me—am I going to hurt her if I grab her?

H.H.: The answer is no.

D.S.: "All right sir, she trusts you, I trust you."

H.H.: Is there something we ought to know that you haven't told us?

D.S.: He only wants people to know, to acknowledge that he is here, he is here. He is whole, he is well—he is here with momma. She is well, she's not quite as happy, but he doesn't know why. She blames herself for his early death—she blames herself. She failed him.

H.H.: How has she failed him?

D.S.: She doesn't think she was a very good mother.

H.H.: Why not?

D.S.: Overpowered, she drank, she drank. She's very sorry. She's getting upset now. What is going on? Is it people from home that are causing this?

H.H.: They have only love for him.

D.S. Maybe it's bringing it back.

H.H.: Any resolved issue between him and the people from home, anything unfinished?

D.S.: He didn't finish his life.

H.H.: I mean in the relationship.

D.S.: There are ties, of all kinds, bringing us back.

H.H.: What kind of ties?

D.S.: He doesn't want to bring it back, he has a lot of hurt.

H.H.: Who hurt him?

D.S.: People hurt him.

H.H.: Who specifically?

D.S.: His momma was hurt.

H.H.: By whom?

D.S.: His momma was hurt by family, something to do with family. They didn't care, she had nothing to eat. I'm sorry. He's going out again—at my shoulder.

H.H.: Don't move.

D.S.: He's leaving, he's leaving. I'm losing him— he's still here, touching me.

H.H.: I don't want him to leave in anger or upset. We will give him some energy.

D.S.: Someone better give me some energy because I'm losing him, he's got my shoulder.

H.H.: Give me your hands, take the energy you need.

D.S.: He's got very big hands.

H.H.: Why is he upset?

D.S.: He doesn't feel this is going the way it should.

H.H.: How does he want it to go?

D.S.: There's been enough written about me. The whole world knows about me. I have no privacy, at least let me have some. Please, please.

H.H.: The reason for the conversation is not invasion of privacy but proof of identity to an unbelieving, foolish, world—nothing to harm you.

D.S.: He doesn't care what they think about him, it is unimportant.

H.H.: It's not unimportant.

D.S.: He wants to know if they can remember singing the gospel songs ... all night long, do you remember?

H.H.: Where?

D.S.: Home, hotels, anywhere, he loved to sing the gospel songs. His momma loved the gospel songs.

H.H.: What about these people present here?

D.S.: He says he loves them. He loves them all. He wants his business taken care of. He wants the people off his property, he wants the garbage stopped thrown about his momma's grave.

H.H.: What garbage?

D.S.: How they do that. He says they're like wolves. He doesn't want this. Get them off his property. That's the only place he had any privacy.

H.H.: What else does he want?

D.S.: He wants his daughter looked after.

H.H.: By whom?

D.S.: Pris, her mother. He wants his father to have some say with Lisa. The only thing he regrets is he wanted his daughter to have a home life. He's afraid she's going to grow up wrong. He's crying. My God, he's crying.

H.H.: We'll do whatever we can to carry out his wishes.

D.S.: His little girl, I'm sorry (starts to sob). He says he's sorry, he's putting me through this and he says it always seems he's saying I'm sorry.

H.H.: What's he sorry about?

D.S.: He can't do anything right, he's sorry he's not cooperating. He's sorry for what he's doing to me.

H.H.: He is cooperating.

D.S.: He says he does not want to upset me needlessly. I'm all he's got, but I'm *not* all he's got. He's always been alone ... and his daughter is always going to be alone (crying).

H.H.: Is there something he wants the two people here to do about all this?

D.S.: Look after his little girl, his baby, his wife—don't let Pris hurt her, he doesn't want her in a boarding school. He wants her to have love. He's all upset. His momma's back.

H.H.: Has she anything to say?

D.S.: She's holding him.

H.H.: Mr. Presley, I will have to release the instrument unless you have something further to say.

D.S.: (Crying)

H.H.: (To the guests) Anything you want to ask him? Then it is best if he withdrew.

D.S.: "No, I'm not leaving Dot."

H.H.: It's best if you separate now.

D.S.: You don't understand, he says.

H.H.: What don't I understand?

D.S.: "We need each other."

H.H.: But we cannot accomplish any more because you are too upset emotionally. It would be best to try another time.

D.S.: No.

H.H.: What does he want to do?

D.S.: He wants people to learn, Hans, that's why he wanted me to see you.

H.H.: Of course they will learn.

D.S.: They are not going to believe.

H.H.: Those who are ready to believe, will, and those who are not, will not. It's their karma—we cannot force them in anyway.

D.S.: (Sobbing)

H.H.: In the name of all who loved you, we ask you to let go, and to separate from your instrument.

D.S.: He doesn't understand why I'm so upset.

H.H.: You're just reflecting his own feelings, there's nothing to worry about.

D.S.: (Shrieks, pain)

H.H.: I ask that the guides come forward and protect the instrument so that the instrument may be released.

D.S.: He says, but I love her.

H.H.: That's understood.

D.S.: "I don't want to leave."

H.H.: You must, for the moment only.

D.S.: "I was left alone. My God, my momma left me alone—I was left alone with nobody. I won't leave here alone."

H.H.: You will be with her again.

D.S.: You're not sending me away permanently?

H.H.: No.

D.S.: For sure?

H.H.: My word—just for now, so that we can refresh ourselves. Go in peace, go in peace, with our love and understanding, with the right to return at all times—go with our blessings, and our prayers.

THE WHALEY HOUSE
GHOSTS
(Westghosts)

I first heard about the ghosts at San Diego's
Whaley House through an article in *Cosmic Star*,
Merle Gould's psychic newspaper, back in 1963.
The account was not too specific about the people
who had experienced something unusual at the
house, but it did mention mysterious footsteps,
cold drafts, unseen presences staring over one's
shoulder and the scent of perfume where no such
odor could logically be—the gamut of uncanny
phenomena, in short. My appetite was whetted.
Evidently the curators, Mr. and Mrs. James Red-
ding, were making some alterations in the
building when the haunting began.

I marked the case as a possibility when in the
area, and turned to other matters. Then fate took a
hand in bringing me closer to San Diego.

I had appeared on Regis Philbin's network
television show and a close friendship had developed between us. When Regis moved to San Diego
and started his own program there, he asked me to
be his guest.

We had already talked of a house he knew in
San Diego that he wanted me to investigate with
him; it turned out to be the same Whaley House.

Finally we agreed on June 25th as the night we would go to the haunted house and film a trance session with Sybil Leek, then talk about it the following day on Regis' show.

Sybil Leek came over from England a few years ago, after a successful career as a producer and writer of television documentaries and author of a number of books on animal life and antiques. At one time she ran an antique shop in her beloved New Forest area of southern England, but her name came to the attention of Americans primarily because of her religious convictions: she happened to be a Witch. Not a Halloween type witch, to be sure, but a follower of "the Old Religion," the pre-Christian cult which is still being practiced in many parts of the world. Her personal involvement with Witchcraft was of less interest to me than her great abilities as a trance medium. I tested her and found her capable of total "dissociation of personality," which is the necessary requirement for good trance work. She can get "out of her own body" under my prodding, and lend it to whatever personality might be present in the atmosphere of our quest. Afterwards, she will remember nothing and merely continue pleasantly where we left off in conversation prior to trance—even if it is two hours later! Sybil Leek lends her ESP powers exclusively to my research and confines her "normal" activities to a career in writing and business.

We arrived in sunny San Diego ahead of Regis Philbin, and spent the day loafing at the Half Moon Inn, a romantic luxury motel on a peninsula stretching out into San Diego harbor. Regis could not have picked a better place for us—it was almost like being in Hawaii. We dined with Kay Sterner, president and chief sensitive of the local California Parapsychology Foundation, a charming and knowledgeable woman who had been to the haunted Whaley House, but of course she did not talk about it in Sybil's presence. In deference to my policy, she waited until Sybil left us. Then she told me of her forays into Whaley House, where she had felt several presences. I thanked her and decided to do my own investigating from scratch.

My first step was to contact June Reading, who was not only the director of the house but also its historian. She asked me to treat confidentially whatever I might find in the house through psychic means. This I could not promise, but I offered to treat the material with respect and without undue sensationalism, and I trust I have not disappointed Mrs. Reading too much. My readers are entitled to all the facts as I find them.

Mrs. Reading herself is the author of a booklet about the historic house, and a brief summary of its development also appears in a brochure given to visitors, who keep coming all week long from every part of the country. I quote from the brochure.

"The Whaley House, in the heart of Old Town, San Diego—restored, refurnished and opened for public viewing—represents one of the finest examples extant of early California buildings.

"Original construction of the two-story mansion was begun on May 6, 1856, by Thomas Whaley, San Diego pioneer. The building was completed on May 10, 1857. Bricks used in the structure came from a clay-bed and kiln—the first brick-yard in San Diego—which Thomas Whaley established 300 yards to the southwest of his projected home.

"Much of 'Old San Diego's' social life centered around this impressive home. Later the house was used as a theater for a traveling company, 'The Tanner Troupe,' and at one time served as the San Diego County Court House.

"The Whaley House was erected on what is now the corner of San Diego Avenue and Harney Street, on a 150-by-217-foot lot, which was part of an 8 1/2-acre parcel purchased by Whaley on September 25, 1856. The North room originally was a granary without flooring, but was remodeled when it became the County Court House on August 12, 1869.

"Downstairs rooms include a tastefully furnished parlor, a music room, a library and the annex, which served as the County Court House. There are four bedrooms upstairs, two of which were leased to 'The Tanner Troupe' for theatricals.

"Perhaps the most significant historical event involving the Whaley House was the surreptitious transfer of the county court records from it to 'New Town,' present site of downtown San Diego, on the night of March 31, 1871.

"Despite threats to forcibly prevent even legal transfer of the court house to 'New Town,' Col.

Chalmers Scott, then county clerk and recorder, and his henchmen removed the county records under cover of darkness and transported them to a 'New Town' building at 6th and G Streets.

"The Whaley House would be gone today but for a group of San Diegans who prevented its demolition in 1956 by forming the Historical Shrine Foundation of San Diego County and buying the land and the building.

"Later, the group convinced the County of San Diego that the house should be preserved as an historical museum, and restored to its early-day splendor. This was done under the supervision and guidance of an advisory committee including members of the Foundation, which today maintains the Whaley House as an historical museum.

"Most of the furnishings, authenticated as in use in Whaley's time, are from other early-day San Diego County homes and were donated by interested citizens.

"The last Whaley to live in the house was Corinne Lillian Whaley, youngest of Whaley's six children. She died at the age of 89 in 1953. Whaley himself died December 14, 1890, at the age of 67. He is buried in San Diego in Mount Hope Cemetery, as is his wife, Anna, who lived until February 24, 1913."

When it became apparent that a thorough investigation of the haunting would be made, and that all of San Diego would be able to learn of it through television and newspapers, excitement mounted to a high pitch.

Mrs. Reading kept in close touch with Regis Philbin and me, because ghosts have a way of "sensing" an impending attempt to oust them—and this was not long in coming. On May 24th the "activities" inside the house had already increased to a marked degree; they were of the same general nature as previously noticed sounds.

Was the ghost getting restless?

I had asked Mrs. Reading to prepare an exact account of all occurrences within the house, from the very first moment on, and to assemble as many of the witnesses as possible for further interrogation.

Most of these people had worked part time as guides in the house during the five years since its restoration. The phenomena thus far had occurred, or at any rate been observed, mainly between 10 a.m. and 5:30 p.m., when the house closes to visitors. There is no one there at night, but an effective burglar alarm system is in operation to prevent flesh-and-blood intruders from breaking in unnoticed. Ineffective with the ghostly kind, as we were soon to learn!

I shall now quote the director's own report. It vouches for the accuracy and calibre of witnesses.

Phenomena Observed at Whaley House By Visitors

Oct. 9, 1960—Dr. & Mrs. Kirbey, of New Westminster, B.C., Canada. 1:30-2:30 P.M. (He was then Director of the Medical Association of New Westminster.)

While Dr. Kirbey and his wife were in the house, he became interested in an exhibit in one of the display cases and she asked if she might go through by herself, because she was familiar with the Victorian era, and felt very much at home in these surroundings. Accordingly, I remained downstairs with the Doctor, discussing early physicians and medical practices.

When Mrs. Kirbey returned to the display room, she asked me in hesitating fashion if I had ever noticed anything unusual about the upstairs. I asked her what she had noticed. She reported that when she started upstairs, she felt a breeze over her head and, though she saw nothing, realized a pressure against her, seemed to make it hard to go up. When she looked into the rooms, had the feeling that someone was standing behind her, in fact so close to her that she turned around several times to look. Said she expected someone would tap her on the shoulder. When she joined us downstairs, we all walked toward the courtroom. As we entered, again Mrs. Kirbey turned to me and asked if I knew that someone inhabited the courtroom. She pointed to the bailiff's table, saying as she did, "Right over there." I asked her if the person was clear enough for her to describe, and she said:

"I see a small figure of a woman who has a swarthy complexion. She is wearing a long full skirt, reaching to the floor. The skirt appears to be a calico or gingham, small print. She has a kind of cap on her head, dark hair and eyes and she is wearing gold hoops in her pierced ears. She seems to stay in this room, lives here, I gather, and I get the impression we are sort of invading her privacy."

Mrs. Kirbey finished her description by asking me if any of the Whaley family were swarthy, to which I replied, "No."

This was, to my knowledge, the only description given of an apparition by a visitor, and Mrs. Kirbey the only person who brought up the fact in connection with the courtroom. Many of the visitors have commented upon the atmosphere in this room, however, and some people attempting to work in the room comment upon the difficulty they have in trying to concentrate here.

By Persons Employed at Whaley House

April, 1960
10:00 A.M. By myself, June A. Reading,
3447 Kite St.
Sound of Footsteps—in the Upstairs

This sound of someone walking across the floor, I first heard in the morning, a week before the museum opened to the public. County workmen were still painting some shelving in the hall, and during this week often arrived before I did, so it was not unusual to find them already at work when I arrived.

This morning, however, I was planning to furnish the downstairs rooms, and so hurried in and down the hall to open the back door awaiting the arrival of the trucks with the furnishings. Two men followed me down the hall; they were going to help with the furniture arrangement. As I reached up to unbolt the back door, I heard the sound of what seemed to be someone walking across the bedroom floor. I paid no attention, thinking it was one of the workmen. But the men, who heard the sounds at the time I did, insisted I go upstairs and find out who was in the house. So, calling out, I started to mount the stairs. Halfway up, I could see no lights, and that the outside shutters to the windows were still closed. I made some comment to the men who had followed me, and turned around to descend the stairs. One of the men joked with me about the spirits coming in to look things over, and we promptly forgot the matter.

However, the sound of walking continued. And for the next six months I found myself going upstairs to see if someone was actually upstairs. This would happen during the day, sometimes when visitors were in other parts of the house, other times when I was busy at my desk trying to catch up on correspondence or bookwork. At times it would sound as though someone were descending the stairs, but would fade away before reaching the first floor. In September, 1962, the house was the subject of a news article in the *San Diego Evening Tribune*, and this same story was reprinted in the September 1962 issue of *Fate* magazine.

Oct. & Nov. 1962. We began to have windows in the upper part of the house open unaccountably. We installed horizontal bolts on three windows in the front bedroom, thinking this would end the matter. However, the really disturbing part of this came when it set off our burglar alarm in the night, and we were called by the Police and San Diego Burglar Alarm Co. to come down and see if the house had been broken into. Usually, we would find nothing disturbed. (One exception to this was when the house was broken into by vandals, about 1963, and items from the kitchen display stolen.)

In the fall of 1962, early October, while engaged in giving a talk to some school children, class of 25 pupils, I heard a sound of someone walking, which seemed to come from the roof. One of the children interrupted me, asking what that noise was, and excusing myself from them, I went outside the building, down on the street to see if workmen from the County were repairing the roof. Satisfied that there was no one on the roof of the building, I went in and resumed the tour.

Residents of Old Town are familiar with this sound, and tell me that it has been evident for years. Miss Whaley, who lived in the house for 85 years, was aware of it. She passed away in 1953.

Mrs. Grace Bourquin, 2938 Beech St.

Sat. Dec. 14, 1963, noon
Was seated in the hall downstairs having lunch, when she heard walking sound in upstairs.
Sat. Jan. 10, 1964, 1:30 P.M.
Walked down the hall and looked up the staircase. On the upper landing she saw an apparition—the figure of a man, clad in frock coat and pantaloons, the face turned away from her, so she could not make it out. Suddenly it faded away.

Lawrence Riveroll, resides on Jefferson St., Old Town

Jan. 5, 1963, 12:30 P.M.

Was alone in the house. No visitors present at the time. While seated at the desk in the front hall, heard sounds of music and singing, described as a woman's voice. Song "Home Again." Lasted about 30 seconds.

Jan. 7, 1963, 1:30 P.M.

Visitors in upstairs. Downstairs, he heard organ music, which seemed to come from the courtroom, where there is an organ. Walked into the room to see if someone was attempting to play it. Cover on organ was closed. He saw no one in the room.

Jan. 19, 1963, 5:15 P.M.

Museum was closed for the day. Engaged in closing shutters downstairs. Heard footsteps in upper part of house in the same area as described. Went up to check, saw nothing.

Sept. 10-12, 1964—at dusk, about 5:15 P.M.

Engaged in closing house, together with another worker. Finally went into the music room, began playing the piano. Suddenly felt a distinct pressure on his hands, as though someone had their hands on his. He turned to look toward the front hall, in the direction of the desk, hoping to get the attention of the person seated there, when he saw the apparition of a slight woman dressed in a hoop skirt. In the dim light was unable to see clearly the face. Suddenly the figure vanished.

J. Milton Keller, 4114 Middlesex Dr.

Sept. 22, 1964, 2:00 P.M.

Engaged in tour with visitors at the parlor, when suddenly he, together with people assembled at balustrade, noticed crystal drops hanging from lamp on parlor table begin to swing back and forth. This occurred only on one side of the lamp. The other drops did not move. This continued about two minutes.

Dec. 15, 1964, 5:15 P.M.

Engaged in closing house along with others. Returned from securing restrooms, walked down hall, turned to me with the key, while I stepped into the hall closet to reach for the master switch which turns off all lights when he said, "Stop, don't move, you'll step on the dog!" He put his hands out, in a gesture for me to stay still. Meantime, I turned just in time to see what resembled a flash of light between us, and what appeared to be the back of a dog, scurry down the hall and turn into the dining room. I decided to resume a normal attitude, so I kidded him a little about trying to scare me. Other people were present in the front hall at the time, waiting for us at the door, so he turned to them and said in a rather hurt voice that I did not believe him. I realized then that he had witnessed an apparition, so I asked him to see if he could describe it. *He said he saw a spotted dog, like a fox terrier, that ran with his ears flapping, down the hall and into the dining room.*

May 29, 1965, 2:30 P.M.

Escorting visitors through house, upstairs.

Called to me, asking me to come up. Upon going up, he, I and visitors all witnessed a black rocking chair, moving back and forth as if occupied by a person. It had started moving unaccountably, went on about three minutes. Caused quite a stir among visitors.

Dec. 27, 1964, 5:00 P.M.

Late afternoon, prior to closing, *saw the apparition of a woman dressed in a green plaid gingham dress*. She had long dark hair, coiled up in a bun at neck, was seated on a settee in bedroom.

Feb. 1965, 2:00 P.M.

Engaged in giving a tour with visitors, when two elderly ladies called and asked him to come upstairs, and step over to the door of the nursery. These ladies, visitors, called his attention to a sound that was like the cry of a baby, about 16 months old. All three reported the sound.

March 24, 1965, 1:00 P.M.

He, together with Mrs. Bourquin and his parents, Mr. & Mrs. Keller, engaged in touring the visitors, when for some reason his attention was directed to the foot of the staircase. He walked back to it, and heard the sound of someone in the upper part of the house whistling. No one was in the upstairs at the time.

Mrs. Suzanne Pere, 106 Albatross, El Cajon

April 8, 1963, 4:30 P.M.

Was engaged in typing in courtroom, working on manuscript. Suddenly she called to me, calling my attention to a noise in the upstairs. We both stopped work, walked up the stairs together, to see if anyone could possibly be there. As it was near closing time, we decided to secure the windows. Mrs. Pere kept noticing a chilly breeze at the back of her head, had the distinct feeling that someone, though invisible, was present and kept following her from one window to another.

Oct. 14, 21; Nov. 18, 1964

During the morning and afternoon on these days called my attention to the smell of cigar smoke, and the fragrance of perfume or cologne. This occurred in the parlor, hall, upstairs bedroom. In another bedroom she called my attention to something resembling dusting powder.

Nov. 28, 1963, 2:30 P.M.

Reported seeing an apparition in the study. A group of men there, dressed in frock coats, some with plain vests, others figured material. One of this group had a large gold watch chain across vest. Seemed to be a kind of meeting; all figures were animated, some pacing the floor, others conversing; all serious and agitated, but oblivious to everything else. One figure in this group seemed to be an official, and stood off by himself. This person was of medium stocky build, light brown hair, and mustache which was quite full and long. He had very piercing light blue eyes, penetrating gaze. Mrs. Pere sensed that he was some kind of official, a person of importance. He seemed about to speak. Mrs. Pere seemed quite exhausted by her experience witnessing this scene, yet was quite curious about the man with the penetrating gaze. I remember her asking me if I knew of anyone answering this description, because it remained with her for some time.

Oct. 7, 1963, 10:30 A.M.

Reported unaccountable sounds issuing from kitchen, as though someone were at work there. Same day, she reported smelling the odor of something baking.

Nov. 27, 1964, 10:15 A.M.

Heard a distinct noise from kitchen area, as though something had dropped to the floor. I was present when this occurred. She called to me and asked what I was doing there, thinking I had been rearranging exhibit. At this time I was at work in courtroom, laying out work. Both of us reached the kitchen, to find one of the utensils on the shelf rack had disengaged itself, fallen to the floor, and had struck a copper boiler directly below. No one else was in the house at the time, and we were at a loss to explain this time.

Mrs. T.R. Allen, 3447 Kite Street

Jan. 7, 1963, 1:30 P.M.

Heard organ music issue from courtroom, when Lawrence Riveroll heard the same (see his statement).

Sept. 10-12, 1964, at dusk

Was present with Lawrence Riveroll, when he witnessed apparition. Mrs. Allen went upstairs to close shutters, and as she ascended, described a chilly breeze that seemed to come over her head. Upstairs, she walked into the bedroom and toward the windows. Suddenly she heard a sound behind her, as though something had dropped to the floor. She turned to look, saw nothing, but again experienced the feeling of having someone, invisible, hovering near her. She had a feeling of fear. Completed her task as quickly as possible, and left the upstairs hastily. Upon my return, both persons seemed anxious to leave the house.

May, 1965 (the last Friday), 1:30 P.M.

Was seated in downstairs front hall, when she heard the sounds of footsteps.

Regis Philbin himself had been to the house before. With him on that occasion was Mrs. Philbin, who is highly sensitive to psychic emanations, and a teacher-friend of theirs considered an amateur medium. They observed, during their vigil, what appeared to be a white figure of a person, but when Regis challenged it, unfortunately with his flashlight, it disappeared immediately. Mrs. Philbin felt extremely uncomfortable on that occasion and had no desire to return to the house.

By now I knew that the house had three ghosts, a man, a woman and a baby—and a spotted dog. The scene observed in one of the rooms sounded more like a psychic impression of a past event to me than a bona fide ghost.

I later discovered that still another part-time guide at the house, William H. Richardson, of 470 Silvery Lane, El Cajon, had not only experienced something out of the ordinary at the house, but had taken part in a kind of seance with interesting results. Here is his statement, given to me in September of 1965, several months *after* our own trance session had taken place.

"In the summer of 1963 I worked in Whaley House as a guide.

"One morning before the house was open to the public, several of us employees were seated in the music room downstairs, and the sound of someone in heavy boots walking across the upstairs was heard by us all. When we went to investigate the noise, we found all the windows locked and shuttered, and the only door to the outside from upstairs was locked. This experience first sparked my interest in ghosts.

"I asked June Reading, the director, to allow several of my friends from Starlight Opera, a local summer musical theatre, to spend the night in the house. At midnight, on Friday, August 13, we met at the house. Carolyn Whyte, a member of the parapsychology group in San Diego and a member of the Starlight Chorus, gave an introductory talk on what to expect, and we all went into the parlor to wait for something to happen.

"The first experience was that of a cool breeze blowing through the room, which was felt by several of us despite the fact that all doors and windows were locked and shuttered.

"The next thing that happened was that a light appeared over a boy's head. This traveled from his head across the wall, where it disappeared. Upon later investigation it was found to have disappeared at the portrait of Thomas Whaley, the original owner of the house. Footsteps were also heard several times in the room upstairs.

"At this point we broke into groups and dispersed to different parts of the house. One group went into the study which is adjacent to the parlor, and there witnessed a shadow on the wall surrounded by a pale light which moved up and down the wall and changed shape as it did so. There was no source of light into the room and one could pass in front of the shadow without disturbing it.

"Another group was upstairs when their attention was directed simultaneously to the chandelier which began to swing around as if someone were holding the bottom and twisting the sides. One boy was tapped on the leg several times by some unseen force while seated there.

"Meanwhile, downstairs in the parlor, an old-fashioned lamp with prisms hanging on the edges began to act strangely. As we watched, several prisms began to swing by themselves. These would stop and others would start, but they never swung simultaneously. There was no breeze in the room.

"At this time we all met in the courtroom. Carolyn then suggested that we try to lift the large table in the room.

"We sat around the table and placed our fingertips on it. A short while later it began to creak and then slid across the floor approximately eight inches, and finally lifted completely off the floor on the corner where I was seated.

"Later on we brought a small table from the music room into the courtroom and tried to get it to tip, which it did. With just our fingertips on it, it tilted until it was approximately one inch from the floor, then fell. We righted the table and put our fingertips back on it, and almost immediately it began to rock. Since we knew the code for yes, no, and doubtful, we began to converse with the table. Incidentally, while this was going on, a chain across the doorway in the courtroom was almost continually swinging back and forth and then up and down.

"Through the system of knocking, we discovered that the ghost was that of a little girl, seven years old. She did not tell us her name, but she did tell us that she had red hair, freckles, and hazel eyes. She also related that there were four other ghosts in the house besides herself, including that of a baby boy. We conversed with her spirit for nearly an hour.

"At one time the table stopped rocking and started moving across the floor of the courtroom, into the dining room, through the pantry, and into the kitchen. This led us to believe that the kitchen was her usual abode. The table then stopped and several antique kitchen utensils on the wall began to swing violently. Incidentally, the kitchen utensils swung for the rest of the evening at different intervals.

"The table then retraced its path back to the courtroom and answered more questions.

"At 5:00 a.m. we decide to call it a night—a

most interesting night. When we arrived our group of 15 had had in it a couple of real believers, several who half believed, and quite a few who didn't believe at all. After the phenomena we had experienced, there was not one among us who was even very doubtful in the belief of some form of existence after life."

It was Friday evening, and time to meet the ghosts. Sybil Leek knew nothing whatever about the house, and when Regis Philbin picked us up the conversation remained polite and non-ghostly.

When we arrived at the house, word of mouth had preceded us despite the fact that our plans had not been announced publicly; certainly it had not been advertised that we would attempt a seance that evening. Nevertheless, a sizable crowd had assembled at the house and only Regis' polite insistence that their presence might harm whatever results we could obtain made them move on.

It was quite dark now, and I followed Sybil into the house, allowing her to get her clairvoyant bearings first, prior to the trance session we were to do with the cameras rolling. My wife Catherine trailed right behind me carrying the tape equipment. Mrs. Reading received us cordially. The witnesses had assembled but were temporarily out of reach, so that Sybil could not gather any sensory impressions from them. They patiently waited through our clairvoyant tour. All in all, about a dozen people awaited us. The house was lit throughout and the excitement in the atmosphere was bound to stir up any ghost present!

And so it was that on June 25, 1965, the Ghost Hunter came to close quarters with the spectres at Whaley House, San Diego. While Sybil meandered about the house by herself, I quickly went over to the Court House part of the house and went over their experiences with the witnesses. Although I already had their statements, I wanted to make sure no detail had escaped me.

From June Reading I learned, for instance, that the Court House section of the building, erected around 1865, had originally served as a granary, later becoming a town hall and Court House in turn. It was the only two-story brick house in the entire area at the time.

Not only did Mrs. Reading hear what sounded to her like human voices, but on one occasion, when she was tape-recording some music in this room, the tape also contained some human voices—sounds she had not herself heard while playing the music!

"When was the last time you yourself heard anything unusual?" I asked Mrs. Reading.

"As recently as a week ago," the pert curator replied, "during the day I heard the definite sound of someone opening the front door. Because we have had many visitors here recently, we are very much alerted to this. I happened to be in the Court Room with one of the people from the Historical Society engaged in research in the Whaley papers, and we both heard it. I went to check to see who had come in, and there was no one there, nor was

there any sound of footsteps on the porch outside.
The woman who works here also heard it and was
just as puzzled about it as I was."

I discovered that the Mrs. Allen in the
curator's report to me of uncanny experiences at
the house was Lillian Allen, her own mother, a
lively lady who remembered her brush with the
uncanny only too vividly. ·

"I've heard the noises overhead," she
recalled. "Someone in heavy boots seemed to be
walking across, turning to come down the
stairway—and when I first came out here they
would tell me these things and I would not believe
them—but I was sitting at the desk one night,
downstairs, waiting for my daughter to lock up in
the back. I heard this noise overhead and I was
rushing to see if we were locking someone in the
house, and as I got to almost the top, a big rush of
wind blew over my head and made my hair stand
up. I thought the windows had blown open but I
looked all around and everything was secured."

"Just how did this wind feel?" I asked. Tales
of cold winds are standard with traditional
hauntings, but here we had a precise witness to
testify.

"It was cold and I was chilly all over. And
another thing, when I lock the shutters upstairs at
night, I feel like someone is breathing down the
back of my neck, like they're going to touch me at
the shoulder—that happened often. Why, only a
month ago."

Mrs. Frederick Bear now stepped forward. I
could not find her name in Mrs. Reading's brief

report. Evidently she was an additional witness to the uncanny goings-on at this house.

"One evening I came here—it was after five o'clock; another lady was here also—and June Reading was coming down the stairs, and we were talking. I distinctly heard something move upstairs, as if someone were moving a table. There was no one there—we checked. That only happened a month ago."

Grace Bourquin, another volunteer worker at the house, had been touched upon in Mrs. Reading's report. She emphasized that the sounds were those of a heavy man wearing boots—no mistake about it. When I questioned her about the apparition of a man she had seen, about six weeks ago, wearing a frock coat, she insisted that he had looked like a real person to her, standing at the top of the stairs one moment, and completely gone the next.

"He did not move. I saw him clearly, then turned my head for a second to call out to Mrs. Reading, and when I looked again, he had disappeared."

I had been fascinated by Mrs. Suzanne Pere's account of her experiences, which seemed to indicate a large degree of mediumship in her makeup. I questioned her about anything she had not yet told us.

"On one occasion June Reading and I were in the back study and working with the table. We had our hands on the table to see if we could get any reaction."

"You mean you were trying to do some

table-tipping."

"Yes. At this point I had only had some feelings in the house, and smelled some cologne. This was about a year ago, and we were working with some papers concerning the Indian uprising in San Diego, and all of a sudden the table started to rock violently! All of the pulses in my body became throbbing, and in my mind's eye the room was filled with men, all of them extremely excited, and though I could not hear any sound, I knew they were talking, and one gentleman was striding up and down the center of the room, puffing on his cigar, and from my description of him June Reading later identified him as Sheriff McCoy, who was here in the 1860's. When it was finished I could not talk for a few minutes. I was completely disturbed for a moment."

McCoy, I found, was the leader of one of the factions during the "battle" between Old Town and New Town San Diego for the county seat.

Evidently, Mrs. Bourquin had psychically relived that emotion-laden event which did indeed transpire in the very room she saw it in!

"Was the Court House ever used to execute anyone?" I interjected.

Mrs. Reading was not sure; the records were all there but the Historical Society had not gone over them as yet for lack of staff. The Court functioned in this house for two years, however, and sentences certainly were meted out in it. The prison itself was a bit farther up the street.

A lady in a red coat caught my attention. She identified herself as Bernice Kennedy.

"I'm a guide here Sundays," the lady began, "and one Sunday recently, I was alone in the house and sitting in the dining room reading, and I heard the front door open and close. There was no one there. I went back to continue my reading. Then I heard it the second time. Again I checked, and there was absolutely no one there. I heard it a third time and this time I took my book and sat outside at the desk. From then onward, people started to come in and I had no further unusual experience. But one other Sunday, there was a young woman upstairs who came down suddenly very pale, and she said the little rocking chair upstairs was rocking. I followed the visitor up and I could not see the chair move, but there was a clicking sound, very rhythmic, and I haven't heard it before or since."

The chair, it came out, once belonged to a family related to the Whaleys.

"I'm Charles Keller, father of Milton Keller," a booming voice said behind me, and an imposing gentleman in his middle years stepped forward.

"I once conducted a tour through the Whaley House. I noticed a lady who had never been here act as if she were being pushed out of one of the bedrooms !"

"Did you see it?" I said, somewhat taken aback.

"Yes," Mr. Keller nodded, "I saw her move, as if someone were pushing her out of the room."

"Did you interrogate her about it?"

"Yes, I did. It was only in the first bedroom, where we started the tour, that it happened. Not in any of the other rooms. We went back to that room and again I saw her being pushed out of it!"

Mrs. Keller then spoke to me about the ice-cold draft she felt, and just before that, three knocks at the back door! Her son, whose testimony Mrs. Reading had already obtained for me, then went to the back door and found no one there who could have knocked. This had happened only six months before our visit.

I then turned to James Reading, the head of the Association responsible for the upkeep of the museum and house, and asked for his own encounters with the ghosts. Mr. Reading, in a cautious tone, explained that he did not really cotton to ghosts, but—

"The house was opened to the public in April 1960. In the fall of that year, October or November, the police called me at two o'clock in the morning, and asked me to please go down and shut off the burglar alarm, because they were being flooded with complaints, it was waking up everybody in the neighborhood. I came down and found two officers waiting for me. I shut off the alarm. They had meantime checked the house and every door and shutter was tight."

"How could the alarm have gone off by itself then?"

"I don't know. I unlocked the door, and we searched the entire house. When we finally got upstairs, we found one of the upstairs front bedroom windows open. We closed and bolted the window, and came down and tested the alarm. It was in order again. No one could have gotten in or out. The shutters outside that window were closed and hooked on the inside. The opening of the window had set off the alarm, but it would have been impossible for anyone to open that window and get either into or out of the house. Impossible. This happened four times. The second time, about four months later, again at two in the morning, again that same window was standing open. The other two times it was always that same window."

"What did you finally do about it?"

"After the fourth incident we added a second bolt at right angles to the first one, and that seemed to help. There were no further calls."

Was the ghost getting tired of pushing two bolts out of the way?

I had been so fascinated with all this additional testimony that I had let my attention wander away from my favorite medium, Sybil Leek. But now I started to look for her and found to my amazement that she had seated herself in one of the old chairs in what used to be the kitchen, downstairs in back of the living room. When I entered the room she seemed deep in thought, although not in trance by any means, and yet it took me a while to make her realize where we were.

Had anything unusual transpired while I was in the Court Room interviewing?

"I was standing in the entrance hall, looking at the postcards," Sybil recollected, "when I felt I just had to go to the kitchen, but I didn't go there at first, but went halfway up the stairs, and a child came down the stairs and into the kitchen and I followed her."

"A child?" I asked. I was quite sure there were no children among our party.

"I thought it was Regis' little girl and the next thing I recall I was in the rocking chair and you were saying something to me."

Needless to say, Regis Philbin's daughter had *not* been on the stairs. I asked for a detailed description of the child.

"It was a long-haired girl," Sybil said. "She was very quick, you know, in a longish dress. She went to the table in this room and I went to the chair. That's all I remember."

I decided to continue to question Sybil about any psychic impressions she might now gather in the house.

"There is a great deal of confusion in this house," she began. "Some of it is associated with another room upstairs, which has been structurally altered. There are two centers of activity."

Sybil, of course, could not have known that the house consisted of two separate units. "Any ghosts in the house?"

"Several," Sybil assured me. "At least four!"

Had not William Richardson's group made contact with a little girl ghost who had claimed that she knew of four other ghosts in the house? The report of that seance did not reach me until September, several months after our visit, so Sybil could not possibly have "read our minds" about it, since our minds had no such knowledge at that time.

"This room where you found me sitting,"

Sybil continued, "I found myself drawn to it; the impressions are very strong here. Especially that child—she died young."

We went about the house now, seeking further contacts.

"I have a date now," Sybil suddenly said, "1872."

The Readings exchanged significant glances. It was just after the greatest bitterness of the struggle between Old Town and New Town, when the removal of the Court records from Whaley House by force occurred.

"There are two sides to the house," Sybil continued. "One side I like, but not the other."

Rather than have Sybil use up her energies in clairvoyance, I felt it best to try for a trance in the Court Room itself. This was arranged for quickly, with candles taking the place of electric lights except for what light was necessary for the motion picture cameras in the rear of the large room.

Regis Philbin and I sat at Sybil's sides as she slumped forward in a chair that may well have held a merciless judge in bygone years.

But the first communicator was neither the little girl nor the man in the frock coat. A feeble, plaintive voice was suddenly heard from Sybil's lips, quite unlike her own, a voice evidently parched with thirst.

"Bad ... fever ... everybody had the fever ... "

"What year is this?"

"Forty-six."

I suggested that the fever had passed, and

generally calmed the personality who did not respond to my request for identification.

"Send me ... some water ... " Sybil was still in trance, but herself now. Immediately she complained about there being a lot of confusion.

"This isn't the room where we're needed ... the child ... she is the one."

"What is her name?"

"Anna ... Bell ... she died very suddenly with something, when she was thirteen ... chest ... "

"Are her parents here too?"

"They come ... the lady comes."

"What is this house used for?"

"Trade ... selling things, buying and selling."

"Is there anyone other than the child in this house?"

"Child is the main one, because she doesn't understand anything at all. But there is something more vicious. Child would not hurt anyone. There's someone else. A man. He knows something about this house ... about thirty-two, unusual name, C ... Calstrop ... five feet ten, wearing a green coat, darkish, mustache and side whiskers, he goes up to the bedroom on the left. He has business here. His business is with things that come from the sea. But it is the papers that worry him."

"What papers?" I demanded."

"The papers ... 1872. About the house. Dividing the house was wrong. Two owners, he says."

"What is the house being used for, now, in 1872?"

"To live in. Two places ... I get confused for I

go one place and then I have to go to another."

"Did this man you see die here?"

"He died here. Unhappy because of the place ... about the other place. Two buildings. Some people quarreled about the spot. He is laughing. He wants all this house for himself."

"Does he know he is dead?" I asked the question that often brings forth much resistance to my quest for facts from those who cannot conceive of their status as "ghosts."

Sybil listened for a moment.

"He does as he wants in this house because he is going to live here," she finally said. *"It's his house."*

"Why is he laughing?"

A laughing ghost, indeed!

"He laughs because of people coming here thinking it's *their* house! When he knows the truth."

"What is his name?" I asked again.

"Cal ... Caltrop ... very difficult as he does not speak very clearly ... he writes and writes ... he makes a noise ... he says he will make even more noise unless you go away."

"Let him," I said, cheerfully hoping I could tape-record the ghost's outbursts. "Tell him he has passed over and the matter is no longer important," I told Sybil.

"He is upstairs."

I asked that he walk upstairs so we could all hear him. There was nobody upstairs at this moment—everybody was watching the proceedings in the Court Room downstairs.

We kept our breath, waiting for the manifestations, but our ghost wouldn't play the game. I continued with my questions.

"What does he want?"

"He is just walking around, he can do as he likes," Sybil said. "He does not like new things ... he does not like any noise ... except when he makes it."

"Who plays the organ in this house?"

"He says his mother plays."

"What is her name?"

"Ann Lassay ... that's wrong, it's Lann—he speaks so badly ... Lannay ... his throat is bad or something ... "

I later was able to check on this unusual name. Anna Lannay was Thomas Whaley's wife!

At the moment, however, I was not aware of this fact and pressed on with my interrogation. How did the ghost die? How long ago?

" '89 ... he does not want to speak; he only wants to roam around ... "

Actually, Whaley died in 1890. Had the long interval confused his sense of time? So many ghosts cannot recall exact dates but will remember circumstances and emotional experiences well.

"He worries about the house ... he wants the whole house ... for himself ... he says he will leave them ... papers ... hide the papers ... he wants the other papers about the house ... they're four miles from here ... several people have these papers and you'll have to get them back or he'll never settle ... never ... and if he doesn't get the whole house back, he will be much worse ... and then, the police will come ... he will make the lights come and the noise ... and the bell ... make the police come and see him, the master ... of the house, he hears bells upstairs ... he doesn't know what it is ... he goes upstairs and opens the windows, wooden windows and looks out ... and then he pulls the ... no, it's not a bell ... he'll do it again ... when he wants someone to know that he really is the master of the house ... people today come and say he is not, but he is!"

I was surprised. Sybil had no knowledge of the disturbances, the alarm bell, the footsteps, the open window ... yet it was all perfectly true. Surely, her communicator was our man!

"When did he do this the last time?" I inquired.

"This year ... not long ... "

"Has he done anything else in this house?"

"He said he moved the lights. In the parlor."

Later I thought of the Richardson seance and the lights they had observed, but of course I had no idea of this when we were at the house ourselves.

"What about the front door?"

"If people come, he goes into the garden ... walks around ... because he meets mother there."

"What is in the kitchen?"

"Child goes to the kitchen. I have to leave him, and he doesn't want to be left ... it was an injustice, anyway, don't like it ... the child is twelve ... chest trouble ... something from the kitchen ... bad affair ... "

"Anyone's fault?"

"Yes. Not chest ... from the cupboard, took

something . . . it was an acid like salt, and she ate it
. . . she did not know . . . there is something strange
about this child, someone had control of her, you
see, she was in the way . . . family . . . one girl . . .
those boys were not too good . . . the other boys who
came down . . . she is like two people . . . someone
controlled her . . . made her do strange things and
then . . . could she do that . . . "

"Was she the daughter of the man?"

"Strange man, he doesn't care so much about
the girl as he does about the house. He is
disturbed."

"Is there a woman in this house?"

"Of course. There is a woman in the garden."

"Who is she?"

"Mother. Grandmother of the girl."

"Is he aware of the fact he has no physical
body?"

"No."

"Doesn't he see all the people who come
here?"

"They have to be fought off, sent away."

"Tell him it is now seventy years later."

"He says seventy years when the house was
built."

"Another seventy years have gone by," I
insisted.

"Only part of you is in the house."

"No, part of the house . . . you're making the
mistake," he replied.

I tried hard to convince him of the real
circumstances. Finally, I assured him that the
entire house was, in effect, his.

Would this help?

"He is vicious," Sybil explains. "He will have his revenge on the house."

I explained that his enemies were all dead.

"He says it was an injustice, and the Court was wrong and you have to tell everyone this is his house and land and home."

I promised to do so and intoned the usual formula for the release of earthbound people who have passed over and don't realize it. Then I recalled Sybil to her own self, and within a few moments she was indeed in full control.

I then turned to the director of the museum, Mrs. Reading, and asked for her comments on the truth of the material just heard.

"There was a litigation," she said. "The injustice could perhaps refer to the County's occupancy of this portion of the house from 1869 to 1871. Whaley's contract, which we have, shows that this portion of the house was leased to the County, and he was to supply the furniture and set it up as a Court Room. He also put in the two windows to provide light. It was a valid agreement. They adhered to the contract as long as the Court continued to function here, but when Alonzo Horton came and developed New Town, a hot contest began between the two communities for the possession of the county seat. When the records were forcefully removed from here, Whaley felt it was quite an injustice, and we have letters he addressed to the Board of Supervisors, referring to the fact that his lease had been broken. The Clerk notified him that they were no longer responsible for the use of this house—after all the work he had put in to remodel it for their use. He would bring the matter up periodically with the Board of Supervisors, but it was tabled by them each time it came up."

"In other words, this is the injustice referred to by the ghost?"

"In 1872 he was bitterly engaged in asking redress from the County over this matter, which troubled him some since he did not believe a government official would act in this manner. It was never settled, however, and Whaley was left holding the bag."

"Was there a child in the room upstairs?"

"In the nursery? There were several children there. One child died here. But this was a boy."

Again, later, I saw that the Richardson seance spoke of a boy ghost in the house.

At the very beginning of trance, before I began taping the utterances from Sybil's lips, I took some handwritten notes. The personality, I now saw, who had died of a bad fever had given the faintly pronounced name of Fedor and spoke of a mill where he worked. Was there any sense to this?

"Yes," Mrs. Reading confirmed, "this room we are in now served as a granary at one time. About 1855 to 1867."

"Were there ever any Russians in this area?"

"There was a considerable otter trade here prior to the American occupation of the area. We have found evidence that the Russians established wells in this area. They came into these waters then to trade otters."

"Amazing," I conceded. How could Sybil, even if she wanted to, have known of such an obscure fact?

"This would have been in the 1800's," Mrs. Reading continued. "Before then there were Spaniards here, of course."

"Anything else you wish to comment upon in the trance session you have just witnessed?" I asked

Mrs. Reading expressed what we all felt.

"The references to the windows opening upstairs, and the ringing of these bells ... "

How could Sybil have known all that? Nobody told her and she had not had a chance to acquaint herself with the details of the disturbances.

What remained were the puzzling statements about "the other house." They, too, were soon to be explained. We were walking through the garden now and inspected the rear portion of the Whaley house. In back of it, we discovered to our surprise still another wooden house standing in the garden. I questioned Mrs. Reading about this second house.

"The Pendington House, in order to save it, had to be moved out of the path of the freeway ... it never belonged to the Whaleys although Thomas Whaley once tried to rent it. But it was always rented to someone else."

No wonder the ghost was angry about "the other house." It had been moved and put on *his* land without his consent!

The name *Cal ... trop* still did not fall into

place. It was too far removed from Whaley and yet everything else that had come through Sybil clearly fitted Thomas Whaley. Then the light began to dawn, thanks to Mrs. Reading's detailed knowledge of the house.

"It was interesting to hear Mrs. Leek say there was a store here once ... " she explained. "This is correct, there was a store here at one time, but it was not Mr. Whaley's."

"Whose was it?"

"It belonged to a man named Wallack ... Hal Wallack ... that was in the seventies."

Close enough to Sybil's tentative pronunciation of a name she caught connected with the house.

"He rented it to Wallack for six months, then Wallack sold out," Mrs. Reading explained.

I also discovered, in discussing the case with Mrs. Reading, that the disturbances really began after the second house had been placed on the grounds. Was that the straw that broke the ghost's patience?

Later, we followed Sybil to a wall adjoining the garden, a wall, I should add, where there was no visible door. But Sybil insisted there had been a French window there, and indeed there was at one time. In a straight line from this spot, we wound up at a huge tree. It was here, Sybil explained, that Whaley and his mother often met—or are meeting, as the case may be.

I was not sure that Mr. Whaley had taken my advice to heart and moved out of what was, after all, his house. Why should he? The County had not seen fit to undo an old wrong.

We left the next morning, hoping that at the very least we had let the restless one know someone cared.

A week later Regis Philbin checked with the folks at Whaley House. Everything was lively—chandelier swinging, rocker rocking; and June Reading herself brought me up to date on July 27th, 1965, with a brief report on activities—other than flesh-and-blood—at the house.

Evidently the child ghost was also still around, for utensils in the kitchen had moved that week, especially a cleaver which swings back and forth on its own. Surely that must be the playful little girl, for what would so important a man as Thomas Whaley have to do in the kitchen? Surely he was much too preoccupied with the larger aspects of his realm, the ancient wrong done him, and the many intrusions from the world of reality. For the Whaley House is a busy place, ghosts or not.

On replaying my tapes, I noticed a curious confusion between the initial appearance of a ghost who called himself Fedor in my notes, and a man who said he had a bad fever. It was just that the man with the fever did not have a foreign accent, but I distinctly recalled "fedor" as sounding odd.

Were they perhaps two separate entities?

My suspicions were confirmed when a letter written May 23, 1966—almost a year later—reached me. A Mrs. Carol DeJuhasz

wanted me to know about a ghost at Whaley House
... no, not Thomas Whaley or a twelve-year-old
girl with long hair. Mrs. DeJuhasz was concerned
with an historical play written by a friend of hers,
dealing with the unjust execution of a man who
tried to steal a harbor boat in the 1800's and was
caught. Make no mistake about it, nobody had
observed this ghost at Whaley House. Mrs.
DeJuhasz merely thought he ought to be there,
having been hanged in the backyard of the house.

Many people tell me of tragic spots where
men have died unhappily but rarely do I discover
ghosts on such spots just because of it. I was
therefore not too interested in Mrs. DeJuhasz'
account of a possible ghost. But she thought that
there ought to be present at Whaley House the
ghost of this man, called Yankee Jim Robinson.
When captured, he fought a sabre duel and
received a critical wound in the head. Although
alive, he became delirious and was tried without
representation, *sick of the fever*. Sentenced to
death, he was subsequently hanged in the yard
behind the Court House.

Was his the ghostly voice that spoke through
Sybil, complaining of the fever and then quickly
fading away?

Again it was William Richardson who was
able to provide a further clue or set of clues to this
puzzle. In December of 1966 he contacted me again
to report some further experiences at the Whaley
House.

"This series of events began in March of this
year. Our group was helping to restore an historic

old house which had been moved onto the Whaley property to save it from destruction. During our lunch break one Saturday, several of us were in Whaley House. I was downstairs when Jim Stein, one of the group, rushed down the stairs to tell me that the cradle in the nursery was rocking by itself. I hurried upstairs but it wasn't rocking. I was just about to chide Jim for having an overactive imagination when it began again and rocked a little longer before it stopped. The cradle is at least ten feet from the doorway, and a metal barricade is across it to prevent tourists from entering the room. No amount of walking or jumping had any effect on the cradle. While it rocked, I remembered that it had made no sound. Going into the room, I rocked the cradle. I was surprised that it made quite a bit of noise. The old floorboards are somewhat uneven and this in combination with the wooden rockers on the cradle made a very audible sound.

"As a matter of fact, when the Whaleys were furnishing carpeting for the house, the entire upstairs portion was carpeted. This might explain the absence of the noise.

"In June, Whaley House became the setting for an historical play. The play concerned the trial and hanging of a local bad man named Yankee Jim Robinson. It was presented in the Court Room and on the grounds of the mansion. The actual trial and execution had taken place in August of 1852. This was five years before Whaley House was built, but the execution took place on the grounds.

"Yankee Jim was hanged from a scaffold

which stood approximately between the present music room and front parlor.

"Soon after the play went into rehearsal, things began to happen. I was involved with the production as an actor and therefore had the opportunity to spend many hours in the house between June and August. The usual footsteps kept up and they were heard by most of the members of the cast at one time or another. There was a group of us within the cast who were especially interested in the phenomenon: myself, Barry Bunker, George Carroll, and his fiancée, Toni Manista. As we were all dressed in period costumes most of the time, the ghosts should have felt right at home. Toni was playing the part of Anna, Thomas Whaley's wife. She said she often felt as if she were being followed around the house (as did we all).

"I was sitting in the kitchen with my back to the wall one night, when I felt a hand run through my hair. I quickly turned around but there was nothing to be seen. I have always felt that it was Anna Whaley who touched me. It was my first such experience and I felt honored that she had chosen me to touch. There is a chair in the kitchen which is made of rawhide and wood. The seat is made of thin strips of rawhide crisscrossed on the wooden frame. When someone sits on it, it sounds like the leather in a saddle. On the same night I was touched, the chair made sounds as if someone were sitting in it, not once but several times. There always seems to be a change in the temperature of a room when a presence enters. The kitchen is no exception. It really got cold in there!

"Later in the run of the show, the apparitions began to appear. The cast had purchased a chair which had belonged to Thomas Whaley and placed it in the front parlor. Soon after, a mist was occasionally seen in the chair or near it. In other parts of the house, especially upstairs, inexplicable shadows and mists began to appear. George Carroll swears that he saw a man standing at the top of the stairs. He walked up the stairs and through the man. The man was still there when George turned around but faded and disappeared almost immediately.

"During the summer, we often smelled cigar smoke when we opened the house in the morning or at times when no one was around. Whaley was very fond of cigars and was seldom without them.

"The footsteps became varied. The heavy steps of the man continued as usual, but the click-click of high heels was heard on occasion. Once, the sound of a small child running in the upstairs hall was heard. Another time, I was alone with the woman who took ticket reservations for *Yankee Jim*. We had locked the doors and decided to check the upstairs before we left. We had no sooner gotten up the stairs than we both heard footfalls in the hall below. We listened for a moment and then went back down the stairs and looked. No one. We searched the entire house, not really expecting to find anyone. We didn't. Not a living soul.

"Well, this just about brings you up to date. I've been back a number of times since September but there's nothing to report except the usual footfalls, creaks, etc.

"I think that the play had much to do with the summer's phenomena. Costumes, characters, and situations which were known to the Whaleys were reenacted nightly. Yankee Jim Robinson certainly has reason enough to haunt. Many people, myself included, think that he got a bad deal. He was wounded during his capture and was unconscious during most of the trial. To top it off, the judge was a drunk and the jury and townspeople wanted blood. Jim was just unlucky enough to bear their combined wrath.

"His crime? He had borrowed a boat. Hardly a hanging offense. He was found guilty and condemned. He was unprepared to die and thought it was a joke up to the minute they pulled the wagon out from under him. The scaffold wasn't high enough and the fall didn't break his neck. Instead, he slowly strangled for more than fifteen minutes before he died. I think I'd haunt under the same circumstances myself.

"Two other points: another of the guides heard a voice directly in front of her as she walked down the hall. It said, 'Hello, hello.' There was no one else in the house at the time. A dog fitting the description of the Whaley dogs has been seen to run into the house, but it can never be found."

Usually, ghosts of different periods do not "run into" one another, unless they are tied together by a mutual problem or common tragedy. The executed man, the proud owner, the little girl, the lady of the house—they form a lively ghost population even for so roomy a house as the Whaley House is.

Mrs. Reading doesn't mind. Except that it does get confusing now and again when you see someone walking about the house and aren't sure if he has bought an admission ticket.

Surely, Thomas Whaley wouldn't dream of buying one. And he is not likely to leave unless and until some action is taken publicly to rectify the ancient wrong. If the County were to reopen the matter and acknowledge the mistake made way back, I am sure the ghostly Mr. Whaley would be pleased and let matters rest. The little girl ghost has been told by Sybil Leek what has happened to her, and the lady goes where Mr. Whaley goes. Which brings us down to Jim, who would have to be tried again and found innocent of stealing the boat.

There is that splendid courtroom there at the house to do it in. Maybe some ghost-conscious county administration will see fit to do just that.

I'll be glad to serve as counsel for the accused, at no charge.

THE GHOSTLY MONKS OF AETNA SPRINGS

(Westghosts)

"If you like golf, you'll enjoy our nine-hole golf course," says the brochure put out by the Aetna Springs, California, resort people. They have a really fine self-contained vacationland going there. People live in comfortable cabins, children have their own playground, adults can play whatever games *they* please, there is tennis, swimming, fishing, riding, dancing, horseshoe pitching, hunting, shuffleboarding, mineral bathing—the springs—and last, but certainly not least, there is that lovely golf course stretching for several miles on the other side of the only road leading up to the place. With all the facilities on one side of the road, the golf course looks like a million miles from nowhere. I don't know if it pleases the guests, but it is fine with the *ghosts*. For I did not come up eighty-five miles north of San Francisco to admire the scenery, of which there is plenty to admire.

As the road from Napa gradually enters the hills, you get the feeling of being in a world that really knows little of what goes on outside. The fertile Napa Valley and its colorful vineyards soon give way to a winding road and before you know it you're deep in the woods. Winding higher and higher, the road leads past scattered human habitation into the Pope Valley. Here I found out that there was a mineral spring with health properties at the far end of the golf course.

In the old days, such a well would naturally be the center of any settlement, but today the water is no longer commercially bottled. You can get as much as you want for free at the resort, though.

Incidentally there are practically no other houses or people within miles of Aetna Springs. The nearest village is a good twenty minutes' ride away over rough roads. This is the real back country, and it is a good thing California knows no snow, for I wouldn't want to tackle those roads if they were slushy.

As I said before, we had not come up all that way for the mineral water. Bill Wynn, a young engineer from San Francisco, was driving us in my friend Lori Clerf's car. Lori is a social worker and by "us" I mean, of course, my wife Catherine and Sybil Leek. Sybil did not have the faintest idea why we were here. She honestly thought it was an excursion for the sheer joy of it, but then she knows me well and suspected an ulterior motive, which indeed was not long in coming.

My interest in this far-off spot started in 1965 when I met Dr. Andrew von Salza for the first time. He is a famous rejuvenation specialist and about as down to earth a man as you can find. Being a physician of course made him even more skeptical about anything smacking of the occult.

It was therefore with considerable disbelief, even disdain, that he discovered a talent he had not bargained for: he was a photographic medium with rare abilities.

It began in 1963, when a friend, the widow of another doctor by the name of Benjamin Sweetland, asked him to photograph her. She knew von Salza was a camera bug and she wanted to have a portrait. Imagine their surprise when the face of the late Dr. Sweetland appeared on a lampshade in the room! There was no double exposure or accidental second picture. Dr. von Salza had used ordinary black and white film in his Leica.

The doctor's curiosity was aroused and his naturally inquiring mind was now stimulated by something he did not understand and, furthermore, did not really believe. But he came back with a color camera, also a Leica, and took some more pictures of Mrs. Sweetland. One out of twenty produced an image of her late husband against the sky.

The experience with Mrs. Sweetland was soon followed by another event.

A patient and friend of the doctor's, Mrs. Pierson, had been discussing her daughter with Andrew in her San Francisco apartment. The girl had recently committed suicide.

Suddenly Andrew felt impelled to reach for his camera. There was little light in the room but he felt he wanted to finish the roll of film he had. For no logical reason, he photographed the bare wall of the room. On it, when the film was developed, there appeared the likeness of the dead girl von Salza had never met!

While he was still debating with himself what this strange talent of his might be, he started to take an interest in spiritualism. This was more out of curiosity than for any partisan reasons.

He met some of the professional mediums in the Bay area, and some who were not making their living from this pursuit but who were neverthless of a standard the doctor could accept as respectable.

Among them was Evelyn Nielsen, with whom von Salza later shared a number of seance experiences and who apparently became a "battery" for his psychic picture taking, for a lot of so-called "extras," pictures of people known to be dead, have appeared on von Salza's pictures, especially when Miss Nielsen was with him.

I have examined these photographs and am satisfied that fraud is out of the question for a number of reasons, chiefly technical, since most of them were taken with Polaroid cameras and developed on the spot before competent witnesses, including myself.

One day in New York City, Mrs. Pierson, who had been intrigued by the psychic world for a number of years, took Andrew with her when she visited the famed clairvoyant Carolyn Chapman.

Andrew had never heard of the lady, since he had never been interested in mediums. Mrs. Pierson had with her a Polaroid color camera. Andrew offered to take some snapshots of Mrs. Chapman, the medium, as souvenirs.

Imagine everybody's surprise when Mrs. Chapman's grandfather appeared on one of the pictures. Needless to say, Dr. von Salza had no knowledge of what the old man looked like nor had he access to any of his photographs, since he did not know where he was going that afternoon in New York.

A friend of Andrew's by the name of Dr. Logan accompanied him, Mrs. Pierson, and Evelyn Nielsen to Mount Rushmore, where the group photographed the famous monument of America's greatest Presidents. To their utter amazement, there was another face in the picture —Kennedy's!

Dr. Logan remained skeptical, so it was arranged that he should come to Andrew's house in San Francisco for an experiment in which he was to bring his own film.

First, he took some pictures with von Salza's camera and nothing special happened. Then von Salza tried Dr. Logan's camera and still there were no results. But when Dr. Logan took a picture of a corner in von Salza's apartment, using Andrew's camera, the result was different: on the Polaroid photograph there appeared in front of an "empty" wall a woman with a hand stretched out toward him. As Andrew von Salzar reports it, the other doctor turned white—that woman had died only that very morning on his operating table!

But the reason for our somewhat strenuous trip to Aetna Springs had its origin in another visit paid the place in 1963 by Andrew von Salza. At that time, he took two pictures with the stereo camera owned by a Mrs. Heibel, manager of the resort.

As soon as the pictures were developed, they were in for a big surprise. His friend's exposures showed the magnificent golf course and nothing more. But Andrew's pictures, taken at the same time, clearly had two rows of monks on them. There were perhaps eight or ten monks wearing white robes, with shaven heads, carrying lighted candles in their outstretched hands. Around them, especially around their heads, were flame-like emanations.

There was no doubt about it, for I have the pictures before me—these are the photographs, in color, of monks who died in flames—unless the fiery areas represent life energy. They were brightest around the upper parts of the bodies. On one of the pictures, the monks walk to the right, on the other, to the left, but in both exposures one can clearly distinguish their ascetic hollow-eyed faces —as if they had suffered terribly.

The pictures were not only fascinating, they were upsetting, even to me, and I have often been successful in psychic photography. Here we had a scientific document of the first order.

I wanted to know more about these monks, and the only way to find out was to go up to Napa County. That was why we were winding our way through the Pope Valley that warm October afternoon.

We were still many miles away from Aetna Springs when Sybil took my hand and said:

"The place you're taking me is a place where a

small group of people must have gone for sanctuary, for survival, and there is some *religious element present*."

"What happened there?"

"They were completely wiped out."

"What sort of people were they, and who wiped them out?"

"I don't know why, but the word 'Anti-Popery' comes to me. Also a name, Hi ... "

A little later, she felt the influence more strongly.

"I have a feeling of people crossing water, not native to California. A Huguenot influence?"

We were passing a sign on the road reading "Red Silver Mines" and Sybil remarked she had been impressed with treasures of precious metals and troubles that come with them.

We had now arrived at the resort. For fifteen minutes we walked around it until finally we encountered a surly caretaker, who directed us to the golf course. We drove as far onto it as we could, then we left the car behind and walked out onto the lawn. It was a wide open area, yet Sybil instantly took on a harrowed look as if she felt closed in.

"Torture ... crucifixion and fire ... " she mumbled, somewhat shaken. "Why do we have to go through it?"

I insisted. There was no other way to find out if there was anything ghostly there.

"There is a French Protestant Huguenot influence here ..." she added, "but it does not seem to make sense. Religion and anti-religion. The bench over there by the trees is the center of activity ... some wiping out took place there, I should think ... crosses ... square crosses, red, blood crosses ... "

"What nationality are they, these people?"

"Conquistadores ... "

"Who were the victims?"

"I'm trying to get one word fixed ... H-I ... I can't get the rest ... it has meaning to this spot ... many presences here ... "

"How many?"

"Nine."

"How are they dressed?"

"Like a woman's dress on a man ... skirted dress."

"Color?"

"Brown."

"Do they have anything in their hands or doing anything, any action?"

"They have a thing around their head ... like the Ku Klux Klan ... can't see their faces ... light ... fire light ... fire is very important ... "

When I asked her to look closer, she broke into tears.

"No, no," she begged off, her fists clenched, tears streaming down her cheeks. I had never seen her emotionally involved that much in a haunting.

"What do you feel?" I asked softly. She was almost in trance now.

"Hate ... " she answered with a shaky voice choked with tears, "to be found here, secretly, no *escape* ... from the Popish people ... no faces ... "

"Did they perish in this spot?" I asked.

Almost inaudibly Sybil's voice replied:

"Yes ... "

"Are the people, these nine, still here?"

"Have to be ... Justice for their lives ... "

"Who has hurt them?"

"Hieronymus." There was the "Hi" she had tried to bring out.

"Who's Hieronymus?"

"The leader of the Popish people."

"What did he do to them?"

"He burned them ... useless."

"Who were they?"

"They took the silver ... "

I intoned some words of compassion and asked the nine ghosts to join their brothers since the ancient wrong done them no longer mattered.

"Pray for us," Sybil muttered. "Passed through the fire, crosses in hand ... their prayers ... "

Sybil spoke the words of a prayer in which I joined. Her breath came heavily as if she were deeply moved. A moment later the spell broke and she came out of it. She seemed bewildered and at first had no recollection where she was.

"Must go ... " she said and headed for the car without looking back.

It was some time before we could get her to talk again, a long way from the lonely golf course gradually sinking into the October night.

Sybil was herself again and she remembered nothing of the previous hour. But for us, who had stood by her when the ghostly monks told their story, as far as we were able to, not a word was forgotten. If recollection should ever dim, I had only to look at the photographs again that had captured the agony in which these monks had been frozen on the spot of their fiery deaths.

I took a motion picture film of the area but it showed nothing unusual, and my camera, which sometimes does yield ghost pictures, was unfortunately empty when I took some exposures. I thought I had film in it but later discovered I had forgotten to load it ... or had the hand of fate stayed my efforts?

Nobody at Aetna Springs had ever heard of ghosts or monks on the spot. So the search for corroboration had to be started back home.

At the Hispanic Society in New York, books about California are available only for the period during which that land was Spanish, although they do have some general histories as well.

In one of these, Irving Richman's *California Under Spain and Mexico,* I was referred to a passage about the relationship between native Indian populations and their Spanish conquerors that seemed to hold a clue to our puzzle. The specific passage referred to conditions in Santo Domingo, but it was part of the overall struggle then going on between two factions among the Spanish-American clergy. The conquistadores, as we all know, treated the native population only slightly less cruelly than Hitler's Nazis treated subjugated people during World War II.

Their methods of torture had not yet reached such infernal effectiveness in the 16th century, but their intentions were just as evil. We read of Indians being put to death at the whim of the colonists, of children thrown to the dogs, of rigid suppression of all opposition, both political and spiritual, to the ruling powers.

Northern California, especially the area above San Francisco, must have been the most remote part of the Spanish world imaginable, and yet outposts existed beyond the well-known missions and their sub-posts.

One of these might have occupied the site of that golf course near the springs. Thus, whatever transpired in the colonial empire of Spain would eventually have found its way, albeit belatedly, to the backwoods also, perhaps finding conditions there that could not be tolerated from the point of view of the government.

The main bone of contention at that time, the first half of the 16th century, was the treatment and status of the native Indians. Although without political voice or even the slightest power, the Indians had some friends at court. Strangely enough, the protectors of the hapless natives turned out to be the Dominican friars—the very same Dominicans who were most efficient and active in the Spanish Inquisition at home!

Whether because of this, or for political expediency, the white-robed Dominicans opposed the brown-robed Franciscans in the matter of the Indians: to the Dominicans, the Indians were fellow human beings deserving every consideration and humane treatment. To the Franciscans, they were clearly none of these, even after they had been given the sacraments of Christianity!

And to the Spanish land owners, the Indians were cheap labor, slaves that could not possibly be allowed any human rights. Thus we had, circa 1530, a condition in some ways paralleling the conditions leading up to the War Between the States in 1861.

Here then is the passage referred to, from Sir A. Helps' *The Spanish Conquests in America*, London 1900, volume I, page 179 *et seq*.

"The Fathers (*Jeronimite*) asked the opinions of the official persons and also of the Franciscans and Dominicans, touching the liberty of the Indians. It was very clear beforehand what the answers would be. The official persons and the Franciscans pronounced against the Indians, and the Dominicans in their favor."

The *Jeronimite Fathers* ... and Sybil had insisted on a name, so important to this haunting: Hieronymus—Latin for Jerome!

How could any of us have known of such an obscure ecclesiastical term? It took me several days of research, and plain luck, to find it at all.

THE DEVIL IN THE FLESH
(Houses of Horror)

If you live in Kansas City you're bound to hear about the Devil now and again, if you are a Bible student or church-goer in a church that goes in for the hell and brimstone variety of preaching. To some people the devil is real and they will give you an argument filled with fervor and Bible quotations to prove that he exists.

Mrs. G. wasn't one of those who was impressed by demonic outbursts, however, and could not care less whether there was a devil or not. She had grown up in a well-to-do middle-class family and spent her adult years in the world of business. At age nineteen, she met and married Mr. G. and they have had a happy life together ever since. There are no children, no problems, no difficulties whatsoever. She was always active in her husband's gasoline business, and only lately had she decided to slow down a little, and perhaps do other things, or just plain nothing when the mood would strike her.

At age 49, that was a pretty good way to do things, she figured, and since she really did not have to work, it was just as well that she started to enjoy life a little more fully. Not that she was unhappy or frustrated in any way, but the gasoline business is not the most exciting activity in the world, and after thirty years of living by and with gas, she longed for some fresh air.

One day in the spring of 1964, a friend suggested something new and different for them to do. She had read an advertisement in the local paper that had intrigued her. A Spiritualist church was inviting the general public to its message service. Why didn't they have a look?

"Spiritualist church?" Mrs. G. asked with some doubt. She really did not go for that sort of thing. And yet, way back in her early years, she had had what are now called E.S.P. experiences. When she talked to a person, she would frequently know what that person would answer before the words were actually spoken. It scared the young girl, but she refused to think about it. Her parents' home was a twelve-year-old house in a good section of Kansas City. It was just a pleasant house without any history whatever of either violence or unhappiness. And yet, frequently she would hear strange raps at night, raps that did not come from the pipes or other natural sources. Whenever she heard those noises she would simply turn to the wall and pretend she did not hear them, but in her heart she knew they were there.

Then one night she was awakened from deep sleep by the feeling of a presence in her room. She sat up in bed and looked out. There, right in front of her bed, was the kneeling figure of a man with extremely dark eyes in a pale face. Around his head he wore a black and white band, and he dressed in a toga-like garment with a sash, something from another time and place, she thought. She rubbed her eyes and looked again, but the apparition was gone.

Before long, she had accepted the phenomenon as simply a dream, but again she knew this was not so and she was merely accommodating her sense of logic. But who had the stranger been? Surely, the house was not haunted. Besides, she did not believe in ghosts.

As a young woman she once heard a friend in real estate talk about selling a haunted house not far from them. She thought this extremely funny and kidded her friend about it often. Little did she know at the time how real this subject was yet to become in her later years!

The haunted house across the street was sold, incidentally, but nothing further was heard about it, so Mrs. G. assumed the new owners did not care or perhaps weren't aware of whatever it was that was haunting the premises.

Her own life had no room for such matters, and when her friend suggested they attend the Spiritualist church meeting, she took it more as a lark than a serious attempt to find out anything about the hereafter.

They went the next night, and found the meeting absorbing, if not exactly startling. Perhaps they had envisioned a Spiritualist meeting more like a seance with dark windows and dim lights and a circle of hand holding believers, but they were not disappointed in the

the messages. Evidentally, some of those present did receive proof of survival from dear departed ones, even though two women did not. At least not to their satisfaction. But the sincere atmosphere pleased them and they decided to come back again on another occasion.

At the meeting they managed to overhear a conversation between two members.

"He came through to me on the Ouija board," one lady said, and the other nodded in understanding.

A Ouija board? That was a toy, of course. No serious-minded individual would take such a tool at face value. Mrs. G. had more time than ever on her hands and the idea of "playing around" with the Ouija board tickled her fancy. Consequently she bought a board the following week and decided she would try it whenever she had a moment all to herself.

That moment came a few days later, when she was all by herself in the house. She placed her fingers lightly on the indicator. This is a plastic arrow designed to point at individual letters and that way spell out entire words. Mrs. G. was positive that only her own muscle power could move the indicator but she was willing to be amused that afternoon and, so to speak, game for whatever might come through the board.

Imagine her surprise when the board began to throb the moment she had placed her hands on it. It was a distinct, intense vibration, similar to the throbbing of an idling motor. As soon as she lifted her hands off the board, it stopped. When she replaced them, it began again after about a minute or two, as if it were building up energy again. She decided there was nothing very alarming in all this and that it was probably due to some natural cause, very likely energy drawn from her body.

After a moment, her hands began to move across the board. She assured herself that she was not pushing the indicator knowingly but there was no doubt she was being compelled to operate the indicator by some force outside herself!

Now her curiosity got the upper hand over whatever doubts she might have had at the beginning of the "experiment," and she allowed the indicator to rush across the board at an ever-increasing speed.

As the letters spelled out words she tried to remember them, and stopped from time to time to write down what had been spelled out on the board.

"Hello," it said, "this is John W."

She gasped and let the pencil drop. John W. was someone she knew well. She had not thought of him for many years and if his name was still embedded in her unconscious mind, it had been dormant for so long and so deeply, she could scarcely accuse her own unconscious of conjuring him up now.

John W. had worshipped her before she was married. Unfortunately, she had not been able to return the feeling with the same intensity. Ultimately, they lost track of each other and in thirty years never saw each other again. She learned from mutual acquaintances, however, that he had also married and settled down in a nice house not far from where she and Mr. G. lived. But despite this proximity, she never met him nor did she feel any reason to.

John W. was also in the gasoline business, so they did have that in common, but there had been difficulties between them that made a marriage undesirable from her point of view. He was a good man, all right, but not her "type", somehow, and she never regretted having turned him down, although she supposed he did not take it lightly at the time. But so many years had passed that time would have healed whatever wounds there might have been then.

When John W. died of heart failure in 1964, he was in his late fifties. Over the years he had developed a morbid personality and it over-shadowed his former gay self.

"Hello," the Ouija board communicator had said, "this is John W."

Could it be, she wondered? She put the board away in haste. Enough for now, she thought.

But then her curiosity made her try it again. As if by magic, the indicator flew over the board.

"I want to be with you, always," the board spelled out now. And then a very avalanche of words followed, all of them directed towards her and telling her how much he had always loved and wanted her.

Could this be something made up in her own unconscious mind? Why would she subject herself to this incursion? For an incursion it soon turned out to be. Every day, practically, she found herself drawn to the Ouija board. For hours, she would listen to the alleged John W. tell her how much he wanted to stay with her, now that he had found her again.

This was punctuated with bitter complaints that she had hurt him, that she had not understood his great devotion for her.

As the weeks went by, her own personality changed and she began to take on more and more of his characteristic moods. Whereas she had been a light-hearted, gay person, she turned moody and morbid and her husband could not fail to notice the change that had come over his wife.

But she did not feel she could tell him what had happened, partly because she did not really believe it herself yet, and partly because she felt it might harm her marriage. So she pretended to be depressed and her husband understood, blaming her middle years for it.

By the winter of 1964, her life was no longer her own. In addition to the frequent Ouija board sessions, she now began to hear the man's voice *directly*.

"I am with you," he explained, fervently, and with her he was. There was never a moment when she could be sure he was not nearby. Her privacy was gone. She kept hearing his voice, sad, but nevertheless his voice as it had been in life, talking to her from somewhere outside, and yet seemingly inside her head at the same time. She could not understand any of this and she did not know how to cope with it at first.

She threw away the accursed Ouija board that had opened the floodgates to the invasion from the beyond. But it did not help much. He was there, always present, and he could communicate with her through her own psychic sense. She found it difficult to fall asleep. About that time she noticed she was no longer alone in bed. At first she thought it was her imagination, spurred on by fear, that made her *think* the undesired one was with her. But she soon felt his physical presence close to her body.

One night she extended her hand and clearly felt *something* other than air above her own body! She let out a scream and turned on the light. But this merely woke her husband and she had to explain it as a bad dream, so that he would not be alarmed.

Night after night, she felt John W.'s ethereal body next to or on top of her. There was no mistake about it. He was trying to make love to her from the shadowy world he was in, something he had been denied while in the flesh. She fought off his advances as best she could, but it did not deter him in the least.

At the beginning of their communication with the board's help, she had still felt a kind of compassion for the poor devil who had died so sadly and rather early in life. But whatever positive feelings she still harbored for him soon went by the board and her attitude turned into one of pure hate.

Nothing mattered in her life but to rid herself of this nightmare and return to the placid life she had been leading prior to the incident with the Ouija board.

John W. added threats and intimidation to his arsenal of evil now. Threats as to what he would do to her and her husband, if she did not accept him willingly. Ultimately, she could not bear it any longer and decided to inform her husband of what she was going through.

At first she was fearful as to what he might say. Perhaps he would have her committed to an institution, or at best, subject her to the humiliating treatments of a private psychiatrist.

But her husband listened quietly and with compassion.

"Terrible," he finally commented, "we've got to get you out of this somehow."

She sighed with relief. He evidently believed her. She herself had moments now where she questioned her own sanity. Could such things be as the sexual invasion of a woman by a dead man? Was she not merely acting out her own suppressed desires due perhaps to middle-age change of life?

She went to seek the advice of a physician.

After a careful check-up, he found her physically sound but suggested a psychiatric examination and possibly an EEG—an electro-encephalogram to determine brain damage, if any. None of these tests showed anything abnormal. After a while, she concluded that medicine men could not help her even if they should believe her story.

Meanwhile, the attacks became worse.

"You will always hear my voice," he promised

her night and day. "You won't be able to get rid of me now."

She tried all sorts of things. Grabbing whatever books on the subject of possession she could find, she tried to learn whether others had suffered similar attacks. She tried her skill at automatic writing hoping it might give the accursed ghost a chance to express himself and perhaps she might reason with him that way. But although she became a proficient automatist, it did not do any good.

The handwriting she wrote in was not hers. What she wrote down made no sense to her, but it was he who was using her in still one more way and so she stopped it.

That night, she felt him closer than ever. It was as if part of his body were entering hers, and suddenly she felt her heart being squeezed and she gasped for breath. For a few moments of agonizing fear, she felt herself dying of a heart attack. The next day she went to see her doctor again. Her heart was as sound as it could be. But she knew then that she had just relived the very moment of his death. He had died of just such a heart failure!

Clearly John W. was a disturbed personality in the in-between world in which he now existed after a fashion. He could not distinguish right from wrong, nor indeed recognize his true status.

His hatred and love at once kept him glued to her body, and her environment, it would appear, unwilling and unable to break what must have been his strongest desire at the time of death.

During their courtship he had appeared as a

good person, unselfish and kind. Now he semed bitter and full of selfish desire to own her, unwilling to let her go or do anything she asked him to.

She enlisted the help of a local amateur hypnotist, but he failed to put her under hypnosis. Discouraged, she lost all desire to live if it meant living on with this monstrous person inside her.

One day she saw a television program on which hypnotic treatment in parapsychological cases was the subject of discussion. Again encouraged, she asked for help and went to New York for an attempt to dislodge the unwanted entity from her body and soul.

This time she did go under, although not very deeply. But it was enough for the personality of John W. to emerge and carry on a conversation of sorts with the hypnotist.

"I want her to go with me, she is all I have now," he said, speaking through Mrs. G.'s mouth in trance.

Later she confirmed that she had been on the brink of suicide recently, and this had not been in a moment of panic but as if someone had actually made her attempt it. Luckily, she had managed to pull out of it just in time.

"Do you believe in a god?" the hypnotist asked.

"No," the entity replied and brushed the question aside. "I told her, she made life hell for me, now I'll make her life hell for her."

"But why do that?"

"No one wants me—I want to cry—you just

don't know what this is like—over here—nothing
but darkness—"

Tears came down Mrs. G.'s cheeks now.

"It's me crying, not *her*," the voice of John W.
said, and then, somewhat quieter, "No one wanted
me as a child . . . I came from an orphanage . . . my
grandparents never wanted me . . . she could have
made me happy but she didn't want to. She's the
only woman who would have made me happy, only
her, but she doesn't want me."

"Then why force yourself on her? What is the
point?"

"I force myself on her because I can make her
miserable."

"You can't force love."

"I have no pride."

"Renounce her."

"I don't want to listen to you. She hates me
now anyway. I'm going to take her with me . . . I'll
get her, one way or another, I'll get her all right."

The hypnotist, patiently, explained about the
freedom of the Other Side and how to get there by
wishing oneself with one's loved ones who have
preceded one.

"This is all new to me," the confused entity
replied, but seemed for a moment to be thinking it
over.

But it was only a brief squint at The Light,
then darkness took over once again.

"I've made her cry . . . miserable . . . she made
me miserable. I don't like the way she's lived her
life . . . "

Suddenly, the personality seemed to squirm

as if from guilt. Was this his own private hell he was in?

"I'm not really that person ... I've been lying to her ... just so I can be around her, I tell her one thing and then another ... "

"Then why not leave her and go on to the Other Side?"

"I want to but don't know how—I can't go without *her*."

The hypnotist tried again, explaining that other souls had been equally confused and been helped "across" the Great Divide.

The voice of the possessing entity hesitated. He was willing to go, but could he see Mrs. G. now and again? Visiting privileges, the hypnotist thought, with a bitter sense of humor.

"Will I be able to come back and see her?" the voice asked again.

But then the demented mind emerged triumphant.

"She hates me for what I've done to her. I'm not going to leave. I can do anything with her. Never could do it when living."

Now the hypnotist dropped the polite approach.

"You are to leave this woman," he intoned, "on pain of eternal damnation."

"I won't go."

"You will be in hell."

"She will be with me, then."

"I send you away, the psychic door is closed. You cannot return."

"I will."

A moment later, Mrs. G. awoke, somewhat dumbfounded and tired, but otherwise no worse off than she had been when she had been put under by the hypnotist.

After she returned to Kansas City, she had some hopes that the power of John W. had been broken. But the molesting continued unabated. True, there had been conversation and the entity now knew at least that he was committing a moral offense. But evidently it did not matter to him, for the attacks continued.

After a while, Mrs. G. realized that her anxiety and abject fear were contributing factors to John W.'s unholy powers. She learned that negative emotions can create energies that become usable by entities such as John W. and when she realized this fact, her attitude began to undergo a change.

Where she had been waiting for his attacks to occur and counting the moments when she was totally free from his possession, she now deliberately disregarded all he did and treated his presence with utter indifference. She could still feel the rage within him when he wanted to possess her, but the rage was slowly cooling. Gradually, her compassion for the bedeviled soul returned and as it did, his hold upon her weakened. He had made his point, after all, and now the point no longer mattered. When last heard from, Mrs. G. was living quietly in Kansas City.

THE GHOST CAR

(Houses of Horror)

Marlene S. is a thirty-seven-year-old house-wife leading a typical American housewife's life—which is to say she is neither given to explorations into the unknown nor particularly involved in anything out of the ordinary. After two years of college, she found that her married life took up most, if not all, of her time, but she is still hoping to get her teacher's degree after which she would like to teach English literature on a secondary level. But with four youngsters —ranging in age from eleven to fifteen—and a husband around the house, time for study is limited. Her husband, Mr. S. is a district manager for a shoe company.

Marlene came from an average Nebraska family and nothing particularly shocking ever happened to her, that is until she, her husband and children, moved into a house in Kansas City that will forever be etched in her memories. The house itself was nothing special: about seven years old, inexpensive looking, with four bedrooms, built ranch-style all on one floor.

They moved into this house in 1958 when the children were still quite young. A few weeks after they had settled down in the house and gotten used to the new surroundings, Marlene was lying awake in bed, waiting to fall asleep. She never could go to sleep right away, and lying awake trying to sort things out in her mind was her way of inviting the sandman.

Because the children were still young, ranging in age from one to five, she had to be always alert for any moves or noises in case something was wrong. Perhaps this contributed to her light sleep, but at any rate she was not yet drowsy at this point and was fully cognizant of what might transpire around her.

Suddenly, she felt pressure at the foot of the bed as if one of the children was trying to climb into bed to sleep with the parents.

Marlene sat up quickly, leaned toward the foot of the bed, made a grab, at the same time saying, "Got you!"—only to find herself grabbing thin air.

She assumed the little culprit had quickly scuttled back to his own bed, and got up and went across the hall to the boys' bedroom. After that, she inspected the girls' room. But all four were sound asleep, tucked in precisely the way she had earlier tucked them in and it was clear that none of her children had caused the pressure at the foot of her bed.

She decided she had imagined the whole thing and went back to bed. But the following night, the pressure was back again and again she grabbed nothing but a fistful of thin air.

It got to be such a common occurrence she

quit checking on the children whether or not they were doing it. She then decided that it had to be caused by her husband's moving his foot in a certain way. Somehow she reasoned that his moves gave the feeling the covers were drawn up against her foot, creating the impression of an outside pressure. Far-fetched though this explanation was, she accepted it gladly. But she kept her foot against his for several nights after this to find out what move of his caused all this to happen.

As her husband slept, she observed, but it got her nowhere: the pressure was still present, but there was no connection with her husband's foot or his movements.

She had hardly accepted this strange pressure in her bed when still another phenomenon caused her to wonder about the house. Near the doorway to the bedroom she heard someone breathe deeply and heavily when there was no one but her around. When this recurred several times she decided to tell her husband about it. He shook his head and said he had heard nothing. She did not tell him about the pressure on the bed, thinking it just too absurd to discuss. That night she heard the crackling of what sounded like someone stepping on cellophane just before she felt the pressure at the foot of the bed again.

She knew she had left a cellophane bag at the foot of the bed on the floor and she was sure one of the children had come out and stepped on it. Again she grabbed but again her hands held only air and the children were all soundly asleep in their respective rooms.

By now a little bit of fear crept into her mind when she came to realize that there wasn't really any rational explanation for the strange noises and especially the heavy breathing.

But she pulled her knees up at night and thus avoided coming in contact with whatever was causing the pressure at the foot of the bed.

For a while, nothing untoward happened, and the family was busy getting on with the problems of daily living. The strange occurrences drifted into the background for a while.

Then one night, several weeks later, Marlene was awakened from sleep by a most incredible sound. It was as if a giant vat of water was being poured on the house. The swooshing sound of water cascading down upon them reverberated for several seconds afterward. Her immediate thought, being just awakened from deep sleep, was a logical one—one of the kids had not been able to make it to the bathroom and what she was hearing was the result! But no: they were all fast asleep in their rooms.

The next morning, she examined the floor. In the boys' room she found a strange liquid spot. It was like water, except much thicker and did not ooze out as water would, but lay there on the floor, perfectly cohesive and round. It had neither odor nor color and when she removed it with tissue paper, it left no trace. Her husband explained that probably the liquid had oozed up from the ground or dropped from the ceiling but her logical mind refused to accept what was obviously not likely.

There was absolutely no rational explanation for either the swooshing noise or the presence of the thick liquid in the boys' room. Several months afterward, a similar spot appeared in the girls' room. Since they had no animals in the house, the matter remained a puzzle.

The house was so new that any thoughts of ghosts were furthest from Marlene's mind. But strange things began to occur. One day, a car securely parked across from the house on a slanting driveway, came downhill and crashed into the boys' bedroom. Luckily no one was hurt.

Not much later, another car from across the street did the same thing, only this time the car went into the girls' room. The owner swore he had put the car into parking position on leaving it. Just as he got out, he saw his car roll down the driveway *by itself*.

This wasn't too reassuring to Marlene. Was some unknown force trying to "get" them? Was there a connection between the spots of liquid in the childrens' bedrooms and the two car crashes?

Somehow the atmosphere in the house was different now from the time they had first moved in. It seemed heavy, as if some sort of tragic pressure was weighing upon it. Her husband did not notice anything unusual, or if he did, he did not discuss it with her. But to her there was an ominous presence in the house and she didn't like it.

One night her husband was working late. She had gone to bed and had just turned the lights out. No sooner had she lain down, than she began to hear the heavy breathing again. Next came the pressure at the foot of the bed. With the breathing so close to her, she was absolutely terrified and did not dare move. Whatever it was, it was very near and she realized now that all her reasoning had not explained a thing. Someone other than herself shared her bed and that someone was not friendly.

But what was she to do? The children were asleep in their beds and her husband was at work. She decided that under the circumstances the best thing was to play possum. She lay there as if asleep, barely breathing and not moving a muscle.

She did not know how much time had passed, when she heard the car drive up to their door. The headlights shone through the bedroom window and she heard the motor being turned off.

"Thank God, Don is home," she managed to say under her breath.

Even though the presence was still close by, she somehow managed to get enough courage to jump out of bed and race to the window. Turning on the lights on the way to the living room as she went by, she reached the window and looked out to the driveway.

Instead of seeing her husband and the family car, she was greeted by the blackness of the night. Nothing. No car.

"This is the last straw!" she almost cried and ran back to her bed. Pulling the covers over her she lay there in terror not knowing what to do next. When her husband finally returned after what seemed hours upon hours, she managed to sob out her story.

"There, there," he said, soothingly, taking her head in his hands. "You've been having nightmares."

"He doesn't believe a word I've said," she thought, between sobs, but she preferred being consoled by a nonbeliever than not being consoled at all.

The next few weeks passed somehow. They had requested a transfer to another location. When it came, she was a new person. The prospect of moving into another house where nothing would disturb her sleep was just too wonderful.

Her husband had rented a big, old mansion in Wichita, where they were transferred by the company, and it was filled with antiques and fine furniture of a bygone era.

When Marlene first saw the house she thought, "Oh my God, if any house ought to be haunted, this looks like one!"

But it wasn't and the house in Wichita proved as peaceful and serene as a house can be, if it isn't inhabited by a restless ghost.

The house was full of memories of its past fifty years but none of them intruded upon her and she lived a happy, relaxed life now. The experiences in Kansas City receded into her memory and she was sure now that it had all been the fault of the house and not something connected with her—least of all her imagination, for she knew, no matter what her husband had said, that she had seen and heard that ghost car drive up to the house.

She sometimes wonders who the new owners

of that house in Kansas are and whether they can hear the heavy breathing the way she did. But then she realizes that it was her own innate psychic ability that allowed the phenomena to manifest themselves when they did. Another person not so endowed might conceivably not feel anything at all.

What was the horrible accident that was being reenacted—from the sound of the water being poured down, to the rushing up of the ghost car? And whose heavy breathing was disturbing her nights?

Many times her curiosity almost made her inquire but then she decided to let sleeping dogs lie. But in later years while living in California, her psychic ability developed further until she was able to hear and see the dead as clearly and casually as she could commune with the living. It frightened her and she thought at first she was having waking nightmares. All through the night she would be aware of a room full of people while at the same time being able to sleep on. Her observation was on several levels at the same time, as if she had been turned into a radio observer with several bands.

Clearly, she did not want any of this, least of all the heavy breathing she started to hear again after they had moved to California.

But then it could be the breathing of another restless soul, she decided, and not necessarily something or someone she had brought with her from Kansas. She read as much as she could now on the subject of ESP, and tried her hand at automatic writing. To her surprise, her late father and her grandparents wrote to her through her own hand.

She noticed that the various messages were in different hands and quite clearly differed from her own. Yet her logical mind told her this might all come from her own subconscious mind and she began to reject it. As she closed herself off from the messages, they dwindled away until she no longer received them.

This she regretted, for the presence of her father around her to continue the link of a lifetime and perhaps protect her from the incursions of unwanted entities of both worlds, was welcome and reassuring.

By now she knew of her psychic powers and had learned to live with them, but also to close the psychic door when necessary.

Meanwhile the house in Kansas still stands and very few tenants stay for long.

UNFINISHED BUSINESS

(Possessed)

Possession for the sake of evil, or for the sake of continuing indefinitely a physical existence, is probably the most feared form of this phenomenon. But there exists a type of possession which is clearly confined in purpose and frequently also in time. In such cases, the possessor takes hold of an individual on the physical plane in order to finish some task he or she was unable to accomplish while alive in the physical sense. Once that task has been accomplished, there is no further need for possession, and the possessor withdraws, continuing an existence in the proper dimension: that is, in the nonphysical world.

Nevertheless, there are aspects of this limited and quasi-intelligent possession that are not acceptable to the one to whom it occurs. In the desire to express a need of sorts or finish something that had been started and not ended, the possessor may overlook the desire of the individual not to be possessed, or to be free of such imposed power. Under such circumstances it is advisable to break the hold of the possessor in spite of any good intentions behind the action.

Virginia F. is an average person of full Irish descent, as she describes herself—of the "Black Irish," those who think they are related to the Spanish Armada survivors who took refuge in Ireland in 1588 and later intermingled with the native population. Mrs. F. has five children and lives in a modest home in one of the largest cities of New England. The house was built in February of 1955 and sold to a Mr. and Mrs. J. S. Evidently the home was far from lucky for the first owner; that owner's wife died of cancer in it after about four years. Then it was rented to a Captain M. for about a year. Apparently the good captain wasn't too happy there either, for he left. The next owners were C. and E. B. Within a year of acquiring the house they filed for a divorce. A short time later, their oldest son was run over and killed by a truck. At that point, the house passed into the hands of Mrs. F. and her family. A little over two months after they had moved in, her father had a heart attack in the bathroom and died on the way to the hospital. For nine years Mrs. F. and her family managed to live in the house, but their marriage was not a happy one, and it ended in divorce in 1970. Whether or not the tragic atmosphere of the house has any bearing upon what transpired later is hard to tell, but Mrs. F. thought enough of it to advise me of it and I'm inclined to think that the depressing atmosphere of a house may very well lead to psychic complications. It could very well be that an earlier dwelling stood on the same spot and that some of the older vibrations are clinging to the new house.

On May 25, 1970, Mrs. F.'s divorce was complete. In the fall of the same year she met another man. Francis and his sister Gloria had visited the house after a club meeting, and from that moment on, Mrs. F. and the new man were inseparable. It was love at first sight. For a few weeks, the two went everywhere together, and then the happiness came to a sudden end. Francis was ill with an incurable disease.

He knew he had not long to live. Instead of a wedding, she helped plan his funeral. The night before he died, he told her he would never leave her and that nothing or no one could ever separate them. He also told her that he would come for her soon. That night he died. And when he died his electric clock stopped exactly at the moment he passed out of the body. For the last day of his life Francis had been attended day and night by Mrs. F. and her two sons, but nothing could have been done to save him.

When the man knew that his time was short, he started to talk with her about death and what he wanted to be done. She had promised him to buy the lot in the cemetery next to his; faithful to his request, the day after she had buried him, February 14, 1972, she bought the lot next to his.

That day, strange things started to happen in her home. There was, first of all, a picture which Francis had bought for her, showing the Minuteman on the Lexington Green. The picture would actually fly off the wall, no matter how many times she refastened it. This happened several times and the picture actually flung itself across the room, making a terrific noise. During the three days between Francis' death and his burial, a little valentine she had given him in the hospital would be moved by unseen hands. Someone took it from a ticket, to which it was fastened by a paper clip, and turned it around so that the side on which was written "Love G." was on top. But no one in the house had done it.

The day of the funeral, Mrs. F. fell asleep, exhausted from the emotional upset. At four o'clock in the morning she woke up to find that a piece of paper she had put in front of her, had been written upon while she was asleep. The words read, "Remember, I love you, Francis."

Realizing that this was a message somehow using her hands to write even though she might not be aware of it, she tried consciously to receive another message by automatic writing a week later. The first line consisted of scribbled letters which made no sense whatsoever. But the second line became clearer. It was a love message written in the handwriting of the deceased. There was no mistaking it.

When she confided in her family doctor, he shook his head and prescribed sedatives. In her heartbroken state, Mrs. F. remembered how her fiancé had promised her a pearl ring for Christmas but had been too sick then to buy it. The matter of the missing pearl ring had been a private joke between them. Two days after the last automatic message, she was putting some things away in the bedroom of her house. Carefully she cleaned the top of her dresser and put everything in its proper place. A short time later her oldest daughter asked her to come up to the bedroom. There, on the dresser, was a pearl. How had it gotten there?

"Do these things truly happen, or am I on the verge of a breakdown?" Mrs. F. asked herself. She remembered how she had written to me some years ago concerning some ESP experiences she had had. Again she got in touch with me, this time for help. "Help me, please, to understand. And if you tell me that I'm losing my mind," she wrote, "then I'll go to the hospital." But if I assured her that she was not insane, she would fight. All she really wanted was to be with her Francis at this point.

Mrs. F. was indeed in a fix. There was nothing wrong with her love relationship, but Francis' promise to take her over to his side of life was another matter. I was convinced that those who were guiding him now would also instruct him accordingly. Gently I explained to Mrs. F. that love cannot fully bridge the gap between the two worlds of existence.

There is a time for them to be joined, but for the present she belonged to the world of the body and must continue to live in it as best she could. When she accepted her true position and also her renewed responsibility towards her children, the hold—which the deceased had had upon her for awhile after his passing—lessened. It was as if Francis had understood that his business had indeed been finished. The knowledge of his continued existence in another dimension was all he wanted to convey to his one and only love. That done, he could await her coming in due time in the conviction that they would be together without the shadow of possession between them.

"I think Heinrich is reliving his life through me," explained the American Army sergeant as a summation of his account of a possessing entity who had been with him and his wife at a United States Army base in Bavaria for several years now. "Heinrich means no harm and will never cause any, as far as I can tell. To put it bluntly, I'm attached to him and hope he sticks around for a long while in the future. Also, he is extremely helpful."

Jack and Gina A. live in Army accommodations in Bavaria. He is a professional soldier, and she is a woman of Lithuanian background, who has had a long history of extrasensory perception experiences. Her ESP has saved her husband's life many times. On one occasion she warned him that his post in Vietnam would be hit by rockets at a certain hour. Far from laughing at her predictions, he took every precaution, even warned his buddies, and sure enough at the predicted hour enemy rockets landed on the post and would have killed them all had there not been any warning. Despite the obvious proof of his wife's ESP powers, Jack as a rational Army specialist takes a somewhat skeptical view of such phenomena and wants to make sure that such events are real and not the result of imagination or wishful thinking. The A.'s have a three-room apartment on the top floor of an

Army accommodation in Bavaria which used to be a German *kaserne* (or barracks). The post had been a military one since the seventeenth century, but it was during the Nazi period that much bloodshed occurred here. It appears that one of the buildings was used to house very young and very old Jewish people, prior to their being sent to be gassed in the East. Among these people was an aged schoolteacher named Heinrich and his two young daughters.

Gina saw this spirit shortly after their arrival to the post. She was able to communicate with him and learned that he had been betrayed by his German wife and had died at Dachau. Because Mrs. A. reminds him of one of his daughters, he became attached to her, Mrs. A. explained. As a result he felt himself obliged to protect the A.'s and advise them, as if he were paying back their hospitality, for the A.'s allowed Heinrich to stay on without any thoughts of exorcising him or sending him away. This was the easier since Gina had already contacted her deceased father who during his lifetime was very much interested in occult matters. According to Mrs. A., her father served as a kind of control and in that capacity he had permitted Heinrich to come into the life of Jack and Gina as an influence secondary to his own.

The building where the Jewish people were kept prior to being sent to Dachau had the reputation of being haunted. None of the townspeople liked to go near it at night. The whole business of such a dreadful place in their midst is

still an embarrassment to the people of this small
Bavarian town. But many testimonies by
townspeople are on record, describing moans and
groans heard from inside the empty building,
when there was no one around. A number of
non-commissioned officers and enlisted men have
also heard the weird noises and investigated them,
again without coming up with a so-called rational
explanation. No one would suspect this peaceful
town, so close to the Bavarian lake area, of
harboring so cruel a past. But the ghosts attached
to various buildings in what used to be a Nazi
kaserne are very much in evidence.

However, it wasn't just the ghosts that
prompted Gina and Jack A. to contact me and ask
me to come and do something about some of the
most urgent cases. There was the matter of Gina's
father and his ring. At first the sergeant denied
the possibility of there being such a thing as a
ghost or even a free spirit. But shortly after they
had moved to their present quarters he realized
that there was someone in the apartment with
them whom they could not see. The unmistakable
impression of another presence made itself felt
almost immediately. When the sergeant denied
that there could be any supernatural happening,
the lights started to act up in a curious way. They
would switch themselves on and off repeatedly in
the bathroom and in the living room. Having the
post engineers check out the wiring yielded no
appreciable results. Then the sergeant found
himself on the floor, several times in a row, without
pillow or sheets although he had gone to bed

normally several hours before. *Someone had pushed him out of bed.*

He and his wife discussed the matter calmly and putting things together he allowed as to the possibility of there being "someone" in the apartment with them. As soon as he had accepted this view the incidents stopped. Eventually Jack learned to tell when the unseen presence was close by and when not. With the help of his psychic wife, he realized that this was the schoolteacher, Heinrich, and that he wanted to work through him, Jack, and that there was very little that could be done about it. At this point Jack was willing to play along, especially since he already had proof of the most dramatic kind that people can continue to communicate after their deaths. Gina had been to a neighbor's house and he was alone in the apartment, drinking beer and reading at the same time. Suddenly, Jack felt that there was someone else in the room with him, and glancing towards Gina's favorite chair, *he saw a short, stocky man sitting in it and looking at him.* Shook up by the intruder, Jack told him to get out. Instead, the man told Jack that he was his wife's father and that he should calm down. He explained that he had come to straighten out some minor difficulties between them and not to cause any harm. Nothing like this had ever occurred to the sergeant, so it took some time for him to accept the presence of a spirit in the chair opposite him. *For an hour Gina's father lay down the law to Jack.* When his fatherly talk was finished, he pointed at a heavy gold ring he was wearing and informed Jack that that ring had been made from a ring he had previously owned. It was his desire that Jack should now wear it. Jack was to write to Gina's mother and request it.

After the apparition had faded away, Jack sat dumbfounded for some time. When his wife returned he reported the incident, describing his visitor in great detail as to mannerisms, haircut, complexion, accent, and even the clothes he wore. Gina confirmed that Jack had seen her father as he had appeared in his best years.

A short time later, Jack's mother-in-law sent along the desired ring. The sergeant has worn that signet ring ever since. When he and his wife had another little argument, he got to know the reason why her father had wanted him to wear that ring. The minute something between them was wrong the ring started to feel very hot on his finger. Even after Jack took off the ring the burning persisted. Only a change in his attitude or discontinuance of an argument would stop the pain in his finger. It became clear to Jack that the signet had established a close telepathic link between the deceased and himself.

I took the ring into my hand, and it looked like an ordinary signet to me. It did not feel hot, and I did not get any other special feelings from it. But then, I am not related to the former owner of the ring, either. Two months after our visit to Bavária, Jack A. reported further on the attitude of his two "friendly" spirit mentors who were working through him. While the schoolteacher had only progressed to level number 2, his father-in-law had already attained level number 4. The sergeant wanted to know whether I had ever heard of such designations. I assured him that I had. At age 24, Sergeant A. readily admitted that he had a great deal to learn not only about parapsychology but about life in general. The army had not yet fulfilled all his needs in that respect. His father-in-law comes to him now more and more sporadically. The sergeant has no trouble sensing his presence with or without the ring. Whenever he is alone and he feels the ring getting hot, he knows his father-in-law is approaching. The conversation is telepathic, but it seems that Gina's father can express himself through the sergeant directly and without any difficulties. As for the second possessor, the unfortunate schoolteacher named Heinrich, all he wants is to be permitted to stay on. Since this relationship does not seem to interfere with Jack's effectiveness as an Army specialist, and since it was his expressed desire not to disrupt the relationship, I could do nothing to lessen the hold the two discarnates have upon Jack. While it is clear that the father-in-law's unfinished business concerns the improved relationship between the two young people and the success of the A. marriage, Heinrich's role is not as clear. But Jack learned through his wife's mediumship that Heinrich knew the area in his younger years, and that he had been happy there. Thus, it is possible that it is not Heinrich's final moment and the terrible trauma connected with it that kept him tied to the spot; instead, his earlier reminiscences may have done so. Under the circumstances he wanted to relive those happy moments through someone who was living in the same spot now. Jack, of course, being somewhat of "an empty vessel" (in the sense that he had not yet formed any strong views or set up positive thought forms of his own), seemed like an ideal receptacle for Heinrich's strongly formulated ways of thinking. But it does seem like an odd combination—a discarnate Lithuanian gentleman, a discarnate Jewish schoolteacher, and a technical sergeant from the United States, *with a single body among them!*

The cases of possession involving unfinished business are usually temporary and almost never end tragically. They can have unpleasant consequences, if the symptoms are not recognized as possession but are treated as some form of insanity. Social and religious prejudice against any kind of psychic phenomena is still so strong in some parts of the world, especially in small communities, that people can very well be railroaded into insane asylums merely because they have shown evidence of psychic communication.

A case of this kind is the story of *Little White Flower.* In March of 1964, Mrs. D., a lady in Kentucky, wrote to me asking for my help in a particularly vexing situation. Due to circumstances beyond her control, she was no longer sure of herself, her actions, and—in the long run—her sanity. Her husband was of no help in the matter, since he scoffed at all manifestations of seemingly supernormal origin. Her sole support (if that is the word), came from her teenaged son Bucky who had shared some of her extraordinary experiences. The

D. family lives in a comfortable house on a hilltop within lovely surroundings. There is a man-made lake ten feet from the front bay window, and, farther on, woodlands create a sense of isolation even though the city of Cincinnati is merely half an hour away.

Six months after Mrs. D. had moved into the house she loved so much, she began to hear footsteps upstairs when there was no one about, and the sound of a marble being rolled across the hall, also upstairs. Anything supernatural was totally alien to Mrs. D., who was and is a firm believer in the Bible and in the religious commandments concerning relations with the other world. She lives in what is popularly known as the Bible Belt, where manifestations of a psychic nature are assigned to devilish influence, and it is not popular to discuss ESP, lest one be branded either insane or in league with evil forces.

Nevertheless, Mrs. D. has a questioning and alert mind, and was not about to accept these phenomena without finding out what caused them. When the manifestations persisted, she walked up to the foot of the stairs and yelled, "Why don't you just come out and show yourself or say something instead of making all those noises?"

As if in answer, an upstairs door slammed shut and then there was utter silence. After a moment's hesitation, Mrs. D. dashed upstairs and made a complete search. There was no one about and the marble, which seemingly had rolled across the floor, was nowhere to be seen.

Mrs. D. deliberately set out to ignore the

strange goings-on. She plunged into music, a field she had studied for two years at the conservatory. She was also working part time as organist of a nearby church. With all this activity she tried to cover up any forebodings of unusual goings-on in her house.

When the second Christmas in the new house rolled around, the D.'s were expecting Bucky home from the Army. He was going to bring his sergeant and the sergeant's wife with him, since they had become very friendly. They celebrated New Year's Eve in style and high spirits (not the ethereal kind, but the bottled type). Nevertheless, they were far from inebriated when the sergeant suggested that New Year's Eve was a particularly suitable night for a seance. Mrs. D. would have no part of it at first. She had read all about phony seances and such, and remembered what her Bible said about such matters. Her husband had long gone to bed. The four of them decided to have a go at it. They joined hands and sat quietly in front of the fireplace. Nothing much happened for a while. Then Bucky, who had read some books on psychic phenomena, suggested that they needed a guide or control from the other side of life to help them, but no one had any suggestions concerning to whom they might turn. More in jest than as a serious proposal, Mrs. D. heard herself say, "Why don't you call your Indian ancestor, Little White Flower?" Mr. D. is part Cherokee and Bucky the son would, of course, consider this part of his inheritance too. A long time ago the Cherokee Indians massacred a nearby white village, sparing only one newly-born white baby. The chief raised her as his own, and eventually she married his son. That was Little White Flower, and the D.'s were descended from her in direct line.

Young Bucky took the challenge and pointing his finger into the air, intoned, "Little White Flower, would you consider being our guide?" Mrs. D. protested that all this was nonsense, and they should go to bed. She assured them that nothing was likely to happen. But the other three were too busy to reply, staring behind her into the fireplace. When she followed the direction of their eyes she saw what appeared to be some kind of light similar to that made by a flashlight. It stayed on for a short time and then disappeared altogether. Quickly Mrs. D. turned on the room lights. The strange light in the fireplace returned however, oblivious of the room lights which were supposed to keep ghosts and other unworthy visitors away according to what the D.'s had read.

Bucky started to question the apparition, which he immediately took to be none other than Little White Flower, his Indian ancestor, whom he had raised from the dead. When Mrs. D. left the room momentarily to turn on more lights around the house, the sergeant noticed that the white light had turned into a mossy green, and clearly discernable outlines in the shape of a human face. They dug into the fireplace and found what appeared to be a red clay substance which turned into fine powder when squeezed. It was not something that had been there before or was connected in any way with the fireplace.

After the son and his friend and wife had left Mrs. D. took the fireplace apart, literally, to see whether there was anything that could have caused the strange light. There was nothing in it of the kind that could have been responsible for it.

From that day on Mrs. D. started to find strange objects around the house that had not been there a moment before. They were little stones in the shape of Indian arrows. She threw them out as fast as she found them. Several weeks later, when she was changing the sheets on her bed, she noticed a huge red arrow had been painted on the bottom sheet—by unseen hands.

It was in the winter of 1963. One afternoon she was lying down on the couch with a book, trying to rest. Before long she was asleep. Suddenly she awoke with a feeling of horror which seemed to start at her feet and gradually work its way up throughout her entire body and mind. The room seemed to be permeated with something terribly evil. She could neither see nor hear anything, but she had the feeling that there was a presence there and that it was very strong and about to overcome her. Being Biblically oriented, she knelt by the fireplace and prayed. She had the feeling of a terrible struggle going on for her body and mind and then suddenly the impression was gone.

For a few weeks she felt quite alone in the house, but then things started up again. The little stone arrowheads appeared out of nowhere all over the house. Hysterical with fear, Mrs. D. called upon a friend who had dabbled in metaphysics and asked for advice. The friend advised a seance in order to ask Little White Flower to leave. She had no doubt that the Indian ancestor *had come to stay and was trying to take over*. The metaphysical lady assured Mrs. D. that Little White Flower meant no harm, that she was pleased that she had been called back from the beyond, and that she liked it so much in the D. household, she just didn't want to leave again. All she wanted was a little attention. "If she's that nice, then take her home with you," Mrs. D. said. "I don't want her."

The relationship between Mrs. D. and Little White Flower was at a stand-off at this point. As the arrowheads appeared all over the house she threw them out. Apparently this did not please the would-be possessor.

Shortly after Mrs. D. returned from church one day, she found that someone unseen had put the thermostat up to 90 degrees. Then she noticed that burned into the hearth brick was a very clear flower, with leaves and graceful stems on both sides. She scrubbed it over and over and finally it was absorbed by lots of fires and overlaying burns. But before she was able to obliterate it entirely she called on a friendly minister to see for himself that she was not imagining things, as he had suggested in conversation some time before. He saw the flower all right, but he could only suggest that Mrs. D. enter psychiatric care. Since she was in no mood to do so, and became more and more frightened that her husband might railroad her into treatment she neither wanted nor needed, she kept her experiences to herself. Only her son Bucky, home again from the Army and evidently psychic himself, was permitted to share them.

Although Little White Flower was not in evidence continuously and seemed to come and go, Mrs. D. felt the Indian woman's influence upon her at all times. She thought that Little White Flower was attracted to her, particularly, even though she was not a blood relative of Mrs. D. She felt that Little White Flower was lonely in the world in which she was, and liked the warmth of a living family. More and more did Mrs. D. sympathize with the little Indian girl's plight. As she did so, she found it more and more difficult to reject her.

Those were troublesome weeks for her. On the one hand, she knew that this entity was slowly getting possession of her, but she felt that there was nothing evil in that. On the other hand, she had been told repeatedly by her minister and by her husband and by a physician friend that dabbling in the occult was either evil or simply a way of getting herself committed to an institution. Under those pressures, she finally turned to me for advice. She had read of me in the *Cincinnati Inquirer*, and thought that I could possibly help her break the hold Little White Flower had on her.

"I'd like to have her exorcised once and for all time," she said. "With regrets, but firmly." My offer to help relieved her anxiety about incipient insanity, but the tactics of her would-be possessor changed as soon as I entered the fray. Little White Flower returned to the D. household with a bang, leaving a stone the size of a chicken egg during a dinner party. Mrs. D. somehow managed to joke over the sudden appearance of this object. Later that night she felt restless, when she suddenly heard a human voice from downstairs repeat four times over, "No, no." She took it to mean that Little White Flower did not wish to be sent away by me. The thought that the possessing entity was worried about my coming pleased Mrs. D.

Later the same week, Little White Flower put in another appearance, this time visual. It was toward four o'clock in the morning, when Mrs. D. woke up with the firm impression that her tormentor was in the room. As she looked out into the hall, she saw on the wall a little red object resembling a human eye, and directly below it what seemed like half a mouth. Looking closer, she discerned two red eyes and a white mouth below. It reminded her of some clowns she had seen in the circus. The vision remained on the wall for two or three minutes and then vanished completely.

The red glowing eyes which reminded her of hot embers and the seemingly laughing mouth were too much for Mrs. D. In a fit of hysteria, she ran to her son Bucky and described what she had just seen. Her metaphysician friend's efforts to make Little White Flower leave by her own volition were a complete failure. The pressure upon Mrs. D. grew steadily as the days went on. While Mrs. D. wondered whether all this was not perhaps due to her overactive imagination, she soon discovered that she was not the only one to experience it.

That week they had a house guest named Nelda and her daughter Delores. At three-thirty in the morning, Little White Flower appeared on the wall, and the three of them saw it equally clearly. This time the face was white and they could make out her long hair, mouth and eyes. After a moment of manifesting in this manner, the face dissolved.

By now I realized that Mrs. D. needed help quickly. But I was not about to rush down to Kentucky, even if I had wanted to, since I had engagements elsewhere. I therefore telephoned my good friend John Strader, a highly respected Cincinnati businessman and amateur investigator of psychic phenomena, to see whether he could temporarily help things and talk to Mrs. D. Jack Strader visited the D. household, listened to her tales of woe, and managed to explain a few things about the phenomena to her. But the phenomena themselves continued.

Early in April of 1964, a Mrs. Dugan, a member of Mrs. D.'s church, suggested that she try automatic writing to find out what the possessor wanted of her. The results looked more like unintelligible scribblings than an intelligent message. But as the words began to take on more and more meaning, Mrs. D. wondered whether it wasn't perhaps due to her own unconscious mind. Her sessions of automatic writing became more numerous. On examining the records, I found that most of the questions asked by Mrs. D. were of the leading kind, that is to say she was supplying information which she wanted either confirmed or denied. Consequently the automatic writing material had absolutely no evidential value as far as establishing the authenticity of the phenomena was concerned. But it became clear to me that Mrs.

D. was becoming too involved in this procedure, and the dialogue between her and Little White Flower was of the kind that could only lead to an unhealthy relationship in which she would be the subordinate taking orders from Little White Flower, whoever she might be, and trying to please the possessing entity in order to have peace. The messages were authentic, however. Mrs. D. did not know what she was about to write until it actually appeared on paper. The thoughts did not precede the writing, as is the case with normal writing, but the hand actually put down ideas which were not in her mind at the time of the writing.

On the other hand, the crude answers allegedly written or dictated by Little White Flower do show a certain familiarity with Mrs. D.'s personal life. Also, the letters, while crude and incoherent, do resemble the handwriting of Mrs. D. to a large degree. Soon Mrs. D. started to worry what Little White Flower would do when I arrived. Far from welcoming my intercession as the answer to her problem, there appeared a curious split in Mrs. D.'s personality. One part of her welcomed the liberation from the influences of Little White Flower, while the other took the interest of the possessor at heart and worried what I might do to her. A religiously oriented friend in whom she confided her problem immediately suggested that Mrs. D. find out if the possessing entity was good or evil. If she was good, the entity would have to be a Christian. Otherwise she would have been sent from "the other place." With the most astonishing naivete, in

view of her past reading, Mrs. D. then asked Little
White Flower, through automatic writing,
whether she was indeed sent by Jesus Christ. She
also wondered whether the Indian girl would hurt
her or her son Bucky, and asked that the Indian
please tell her what her intentions were. When
Mrs. D. failed to obtain any satisfactory replies to
these questions, she wrote in a pique, "I'm not going to write to you anymore. I've tried helping you
and so has Bucky and Mr. Holzer." But she did not
take her own threat seriously. On May 23, 1964,
she resumed the correspondence with her tormentor. This time Little White Flower, or whatever
was guiding Mrs. D.'s hand, replied that she had
some news for *Mrs.* Holzer. Mrs. Holzer was missing a diamond brooch. That brooch was situated in
the grave of a certain Matthew in a cemetery in
Richmond, Virginia.

Not only was Mrs. Holzer not missing any
diamond brooch, but she does not own one. It was
clear to me that these messages were merely statements of a quasi-evidential nature. That is,
sounding as if they could be followed up, but at the
same time so designed that it would take a great
deal of effort and time to prove or disprove them. I
wondered whether they came from a separate entity or were not in fact part of Mrs. D.'s own
unconscious mind and an expression of her dissat-
isfaction with the automatic correspondence. At
the same time she began to doubt the authenticity
of this dialogue between herself and Little White
Flower altogether.

After several postponements I was finally

able to come to Kentucky and meet with Mrs. D. in person. On June 20, 1964, I sat opposite the slightly portly, middle-aged lady who had corresponded with me for several months and so voluminously. There was nothing odd or weird about her appearance or speech. Anyone suspecting Mrs. D. of incipient insanity was off the mark. It was a quiet warm afternoon and I decided to use my time intelligently. We were alone in the house so I suggested that we seat ourselves in front of the fireplace and try to recreate as much as possible of the original seance where Little White Flower had put in her first appearance. This done, we waited quietly for something to happen. After two or three minutes of silence, Mrs. D. intoned, "She's here."

I neither saw nor felt anything special but Mrs. D. immediately broke into tears, weeping for her unseen friend and possessor. She complained of feeling heavy on top of her head and somehow "crowded" within her own body. She felt squashed, as if there were someone else within her, pushing her own self to one side.

It occurred to me that the possessor had some unfinished business that had nothing to do with Mrs. D., and that she was merely using her as an open channel to express a grievance or desire. Had the entity been properly buried, for instance? I wondered. There was no answer, so I continued to admonish the unseen entity that the D. home was not hers, and that she was to leave the occupants alone. With a voice filled with as much authority as I could muster in the hot June weather, I then sent her away, back to her own world, and forbade her any further intercourse with the D. family. This was, of course, done as much for the benefit of Little White Flower as for Mrs. D. It is my experience that exorcism works best when the one being exorcised is equally sure of being freed of the possessing entity as the possessing entity is as sure of being separated from his or her earthly partner. Anyone who wishes to read psychological overtones into this technique may do so. The fact remains that a firm conviction that someone is doing something about one's problem is unquestionably a helpful agent and may, in some as yet not fully understood way, help dispatch the possessing entity. But make no mistake about it, in this case as well as in many others, there was an actual possessor involved and Little White Flower was no more the figment of the imagination than were the little arrow-shapes and other apports so generously bestowed upon the D. household over the past two years.

As I intoned my solemn exorcism and demanded Little White Flower's withdrawal from the spot, I could hear Mrs. D. crying hysterically. It was almost as if some part of her was being torn out and for a while it seemed that *she* was being sent away, not Little White Flower.

As for Mr. D., he couldn't care less what was done to his great-great-grandmother. All he wanted was for his wife to be free from "her troubles."

Six days later, on June 26, Mrs. D. wrote me another letter. It was filled with expressions of gratitude and sounded totally different from her previous communications to me. "Things are so peaceful around here since you helped Little White Flower back to her own people," she wrote, "We extend to you an open invitation to stay with us whenever you are in this territory."

On August 13, 1964, she reported to me once again. "Everything has been quiet and nice since you told me what to do." That prescription included a firm *no-no* concerning automatic writing, Ouija boards, and any other traffic with the unseen. There was no telling what Mrs. D., with her proven psychic talents, might conjure up the next time she tried her hand at it.

POSSESSION AND OBSESSION

(Possessed)

"The man/woman is possessed," or "Whatever possessed him/her?" are popular phrases describing a person who doesn't act quite like him or herself—that is to say, a person with marked personality changes so obvious that everyone can see them. "Possessed by the furies" is a more poetic way of expressing the thought that a person is being led by some form of madness.

Take Jane X. She's an ordinary housewife. She lives with her husband and three children in a suburb of one of America's largest cities. She is thirty years old, has never had the slightest interest in occult matters, goes to church whenever she can't escape going, reads very little, and then only reads subjects of average nature. One fine day Jane starts behaving like a totally different person. She has new ideas, knowledge of places or situations she couldn't possibly have seen, and even her facial expressions are no longer her own. Gradually she speaks with someone else's tongue. Not only does she say things that she couldn't possibly say when she was just plain Jane, but she reacts differently to the world around her. Gradually her behavior becomes so unusual that a physician is called in. After carefully investigating the circumstances, the physician will probably recommend that a psychiatrist be called into the case. The psychiatrist will question the new Jane. After a while he or she will come to the conclusion that Jane has suffered a nervous breakdown or perhaps, even worse, exhibits signs of schizophrenia or split personality. Treatment in an institution or private analysis may be recommended depending upon the situation.

Jack S. is a well-to-do sales manager for an Eastern company. He's been married for twenty-two years, has a happy home life, nice hobbies, and really no problems. One fine day he enters a local restaurant, takes out a gun and shoots four people he has never met before. Afterwards, he remembers absolutely nothing. He is routinely sentenced to a long jail term, branded a wanton murderer, and still another unsolved crime goes into the records. To the criminologist, to the physician, to the judge, this is merely a case of sudden insanity—criminal insanity perhaps, but without any unusual overtones. Some of these cases certainly are. Some are not. What I have just mentioned are two classic cases of *possession*. They are not actual cases, and the names mentioned are fictitious, but I can match these hypothetical cases over and over with real stories from my files. The purpose of crystallizing here two of the most serious forms possession can take is to bring out how easy it is to fall prey to misconceptions regarding possession. Possession can be masked in many ways. This does not mean that one should become hysterical and look for real possession in every case of personality change or whenever someone acts strangely. Nothing would be further from the purpose of this report. I do not wish to alarm anyone or to start an entire movement of "possession hunters" in the fashion of the medieval witch hunters. Generally speaking, actual cases are rarely as defined and as clear-cut as the two main examples I have just quoted. I will go into the specifics of each case when necessary, but suffice it to say that possession follows no simple law. That is to say, it may follow many laws of which we are only dimly aware. It can come suddenly or gradually. It can come partially or totally. It can even disappear at times without anyone doing anything about it, although *that* is decidedly rare.

The word possession comes from the Latin *possedere*, which means, quite obviously, "to possess, to own, to take over." Taking the word's two components, however, we find possession consisting of *post* and *sedere*. The latter word means "to sit, to be situated," and the "post" generally stands for "after" or "beyond." Thus, when we translate freely *possedere* means "to sit on top of." It is interesting to note in this connection that in the Middle Ages, a popular conception of possession included a wraith or gnome sitting on top of the possessed individual, pushing down upon his or her body, causing nightmares and other forms of altered states of consciousness. The concept of the word *possession* indicates that it relates to a total takeover, and total control of an individual by another individual or some outside force. Possession excludes the will of the possessed. It presupposes the inability of the victim to overcome the attacking force and in submitting to it, becomes its tool.

What exactly is possession in terms of various approaches? We can distinguish between the medical, religious, popular, and, finally, parapsychological approach to the problem of possession. In a *medical sense*, the verdict is likely to be schizophrenia or some other form of mental or even physical derangement. The medical profession on the whole does not acknowledge the existence of separate entities apart from the flesh-and-blood personality of the victim. In fact, medical experts barely recognize the possibility that humans have something more than a physical body. Medicine has as yet not come to terms with the entire problem of human personality-soul-spirit. In medical terms then, the possibility of one person being possessed by another against his or her will is entirely inconceivable, with the sole marginal exception of hypnosis, of course, or some other form of undue but direct influence. When a person shows marked personality changes and acts in a way contrary to his or her previous habits, the medical doctor will look for personality defects rather than the presence of a new or outside personality. With the advent of psychiatry, the reality of secondary and even tertiary personalities within the personality complex of one human being has become an accepted fact. But these secondary and tertiary personalities are still considered parts of the original personality, and in the view of most medical men, such parts must be reunited with the main personality or entirely destroyed if the patient is to become well again. A celebrated case in point was the case later dramatized as *The Three Faces of Eve*, in which such split-off parts of personality were dealt with in great detail. The medical doctors dealing with the case at the time came to the conclusion that the second and third personalities displayed by Eve were in fact only underlying split-off parts of Eve's own self in the end.

I have, on careful study of this and similar cases, come to the conclusion that this is not necessarily the answer but that there may be another parapsychological explanation for the strange personality splits within one individual as shown in the case of *The Three Faces of Eve*. The possibility of interference from a dimension other than the physical one must not be discounted. This holds particularly true in instances where the individual displays amazing skills and abilities incompatible with his or her upbringing, training, and general background. Some medical experts and especially psychiatrists like to explain this as latent abilities always present but dormant in the individual, abilities which are awakened by the process of splitting-off secondary personalities. But this does not seem to be a satisfactory explanation, since many such talents could not possibly have been dormant in the individuals concerned and could not have been acquired by osmosis or in some marginal fashion. For instance, the ability to speak a foreign language with great fluency or the ability to drive a car when the individual has had no training whatsoever in either of these areas—this cannot simply be explained by dormant talents present all the time within the individual. Such skill must enter the conscious or unconscious of the person somewhere along the line, and this has not been the case in a number of instances known to me. The only logical explanation for such behavior seems to me to be the transference of knowledge or skills from the outside; that is to say, by an outside entity functioning in another dimension. To put it into the vernacular, I am convinced that in certain cases of this type, in which secondary and other multiple personalities have occurred, there exists a situation wherein a living individual with full consciousness, but functioning in a nonphysical dimension, operates the body and mind of a living person. This relationship between a deceased mind and a living mind may be contrary to orthodox medical view, but the evidence points strongly in the direction that such a relationship does, in fact, exist.

Possession in terms of the *religious establishment* is nothing but the entrance into the soul of the concerned individual of an outside force, generally evil. Whether or not the term demonic possession is used, the inference is that a living entity has entered the body of the victim in order to express his or her own will and frustrations. To the church, this is always evil and must be dealt with through exorcists. Not every religious community accepts this version, but the so-called orthodox faiths do believe in the existence of possession and the need for exorcism. To this day, the Catholic Church retains the rite of exorcism in its Scriptures. In an offshoot of orthodox Judaism called the Chasidic cult, belief in the *dybbuk* or possessing spirit is still extant and is dealt with similarly as in the Roman Catholic exorcism. In both cases, the possessing spirit is asked to leave and when it refuses, forced out of the body of the victim by various means. In bygone days these means included everything from torture to bizarre threats and incantations believed to be effective by the sheer power of the arrangement of phrases. When only words were used to drive out the evil spirits the matter had either no effect or, through a form of hypnotic suggestion, resulted in freeing the victim from its possessor. However, when physical torture was used and applied (in theory to the possessing entity, but in practice hurting the victim) the results were not as fortunate. The church believed that the death of a possessed individual in the process of trying to free that person from its possessor was unavoidable if the evil spirit was stronger than the victim. The church felt that it was better to destroy both than permit the victim to exist under the spell of its possessor and possibly harm others. The number of unfortunate people who were thus tortured to death by seemingly well-meaning exorcists of religious background is considerable.

In terms of modern psychology, this is what happened. The priest or minister held himself up as the representative of the forces of God and of good faced with the presence of what he considered an evil spirit in the hapless body of the victim. He overlooked entirely the victim's own involvement in the matter and considered it strictly an affair between himself and the devil represented by the evil spirit possessing the victim in front of him. With every blow struck against the possessing entity, the exorcist's religious fanaticism rose to new heights, and if the body of the possessed expired in the process, well, at least the soul was now free to go up to heaven and worry no more about being possessed. On the earth level, the exorcist could rightly claim victory over another demon. The church had once again proven its superiority over the forces of darkness! This was psychologically satisfactory to the exorcist in that it reconfirmed his divine mission in driving out demons at all costs. But we must never forget that the true fanatic is lacking in self-respect and personal emotional security. He seeks his fulfillment in the imposition of his views or ideology upon others. Rather than seeking individual acclaim, he prefers being an instrument for some large force for good or other ideological concept; in this force, he is merely one small part or tool. Thus he obtains personal emotional security from the knowledge, true or false, that there are many others like him who agree with him and support his actions. If the exorcist succeeded, it had to be proven by the victim's rational behavior, but in terms of religious exorcism, it was also proven by the victim's further relationship with the church and God. If the victim showed any changes from his or her previous attitude in this respect, or if the victim deviated even in the slightest from the official line, the exorcism could not be called successful.

If the victim survived religious exorcism with its possessor intact, then clearly the exorcist had but two choices: destroy the victim altogether and thus take care of both the victim and possessor, or to place the victim into permanent confinement where he or she could do no harm to others, in the view of the exorcist. At the same time, the victim became available to the "forces of mercy," should these forces decide to rescue the victim, after all, without benefit of the exorcist. Thus, countless wretches, whose sole problem had been possession, were thrust into dungeons under the supervision of the Inquisition or the church in general, and expired eventually through neglect.

The popular attitude towards possession combines certain elements of the religious and medical approaches, but adds another dimension—that of fear and superstition. Both physicians and churchmen knew very well that touching the body of a possessed individual could have no dire consequences for them, since the body belonged to the victim and not to the possessor. But in the popular view, the very touch of the possessed was poisonous and had to be avoided at all costs. Being in the presence of a possessed person and looked at by such an individual could also have terrible consequences. In the southern part of Europe, this popular superstition became confused with the evil eye concept, and people thought that the casting of glances by a possessed person upon a healthy one was in itself sufficient grounds for a healthy person to fall ill and perhaps become possessed him or herself. In antiquity, it was frequently customary to drive a possessed person out of town, with the idea that so long as the individual was no longer in the immediate vicinity, one couldn't care less where else the possessed one might cause damage. Driving the possessed from the confines of one's village eventually led to chasing the victim out, but stoning the individual at the same time, in the hope that a lucky stone might finish the person off altogether. In that case, the stone that made the perfect hit was not thrown by the individual actually throwing it, but directed by some *superior force* from above and thus entirely acceptable as the hand of fate. Whenever a person who had the earmarks of the possessed entered the community, he or she had to be avoided at all costs. "Possessed by the furies" was the term used for such individuals who were thought to be the victims of evil spirits because of some evil deed they themselves had done.

That evil invites evil is a concept still prevalent among many primitive people and even among many not-so-primitive ones. Anything a possessed person had touched had to be destroyed immediately. In extreme cases, if the possessed had touched another human being, the village would have to destroy that human being, or at least ostracize him or her, lest the entire community be affected. In some respects, therefore, possession was considered by society as a communicable problem, a disease, something one could catch from the victim if one wasn't careful. Under no circumstances could or should one undertake anything to fight against possession. To help the possessed individual was out of the question. The results could only be negative and involve innocents in the process of possession.

Fear, along with total misconception regarding what possession was, helped create a false image in the popular mind. Ever since the established church had made it into the work of the devil during the twelfth and thirteenth centuries, the popular version of what happened to the victim included some form of diabolical influence. Whether it was a demon or underling of the devil, or the Great One himself, inevitably there was at work some hellish play that created the dismal state of possession in the victim. It never occurred to the popular mind that possession could also be the result of benevolent interference or anything less than devilish machinations. Anyone acting under the influence of another individual had to be possessed by the devil and his minions. To the church, of course, such popular attitudes were pleasing, since they helped reinforce her own hold, which had been carefully nurtured over the centuries by threats of fear, upon the people. Threats that sprang from the official dogmatic line promised dire consequences for one's soul, and fear of contact with those clearly not in God's grace would have similar results for oneself.

Only with the advent of *parapsychology as a serious scientific form of inquiry* has possession as a phenomenon of the human personality been brought into an objective focus devoid of all religious prejudices and medical condemnation. The phenomenon emerges as an intensely human, but at the same time paranormal, experience possible only through the interrelationship of two entities. These two entities may be both of the physical world or, as in the majority of cases, in the physical and the nonphysical world.

But in each and every case of true possession we are dealing *with two separate individuals* no matter how restricted or structured in their individual consciousness.

Originally parapsychology also tended to consider the phenomena involving possession as part of the as yet unchartered depths of human personality. Indeed, to this very day, there are some parapsychologists who cannot get themselves to accept the reality of nonphysical entities existing in another dimension than earth. These parapsychologists prefer to force the phenomena of possession into the narrow channels of one-entity concepts. To them, possession involves only abnormal activities of the mind in terms of mental illness. What these parapsychologists suggest, however, as a possible explanation of possession, is a kind of extension of human personality beyond the boundaries presently known. Under this extension, the human personality becomes aware of knowledge, abilities, and other evidential material from beyond its own confines. Such an explanation of possession is, to my mind, a tortured one, and it does not cover some of the incidents involved in some possession cases which cannot be explained on such a basis. These cases clearly involve a completely alien personality which is frequently in total conflict with the rest of the personality, as evidenced by the personality's behavior, both normal and under possession. Again, to put it into the vernacular, to such parapsychologists the victim manufactures the possession entity out of his or her own unconscious, for various reasons. These reasons may involve the desire to manifest greater popularity or interest and register more strongly with the environment, or they may stem from emotional problems and indicate merely the individual's desire to express a greater variety of traits than the individual does in the full conscious state. With this explanation, a possessing entity again becomes a subordinate part of the personality, similar to the conventional explanation so frequently offered by orthodox psychiatrists. The only difference here is that the psychiatrist regards such splitting of personality essentially a malignant process, whereas the parapsychologists considers this a positive factor, indicating greater personality potentials in the individual concerned, and not necessarily a form of mental illness.

In order to understand fully the balanced

approach taken by the more progressive of parapsychologists today (among whom I dare count myself), it is necessary to explain briefly what *the spiritualist approach* to possession is. I have not classed this view among religious approaches since spiritualism is not entirely a religious faith but consists of religious elements along with scientifically based conclusions; thus, spiritualism should occupy a place of its own somewhere between religion and science. In spiritualism, which is considered a religion by some and an adjunct to their own religions by others, the facts of possession are fully accepted. They are ascribed to the interference of deceased individuals in need of further expression through living bodies and minds. Possession is considered an undesirable situation by spiritualists, something that has to be dealt with by experienced operators. But the spiritualist does not exorcise the way a priest does. The spiritualist suggests to the possessing spirit that the spirit's proper place is not within the body and mind of a living human being but in the world of spirit which lies just beyond. In suggesting this, the spiritualist operator then proceeds to request that the possessing spirit mend its ways and go on to the next world. If this is not done, the spiritualist will cite the dangers which the possessing entity is bringing upon him or herself by remaining where he or she clearly does not belong and is not wanted. Moralistic principles are involved here and the enticements of the spirit world just beyond the gates are again brought into focus. If all this fails, the spiritualist will invoke the "powers of spirit," which is a term generally used to refer to the orderly government of the spirit world, and with the powers' help will *order* the possessing spirit to depart. In this respect, this is certainly a form of exorcism, although there are none of the physical aspects of it so dear to the church of the Middle Ages, nor is there any threat of loss of eternal salvation involved as it is with the church rite. This is perhaps due to the theory of spiritualism: that the possessing entity is confused in its aims. With the traditional church's approach, the possessing entity is clearly the evil one and the victim totally innocent. That this is not the case in reality will be shown very shortly. To the spiritualist, it is important to put everyone where he or she belongs—possessing entity into the spirit world, and possessed back into healthy circulation among his or her peers on earth. To accomplish this, the spiritualist may or may not invoke the deity or Christ, depending upon his particular shade of spiritualism, for there are many denominations among spiritualists as well. Since spiritualists do not believe in the devil, they treat the possessor as an erring spirit, somehow gone astray but worthy of salvation, rather than as a servant of the devil, or the devil himself, as the Church does. The spiritualist is imbued with his or her belief in the reality of "summerland," the spirit world, and the orderly way of life in it in which there is essentially only good and no evil and in which "spirit" controls everything on earth, including people. He does not enter into the more complex realms of the human unconscious, of motivation, and of the *duality* of relationship which, as will be shown shortly, is at the base of all possession. In spiritualistic terms, any spirit overstepping the boundaries of communication with the living to prove continued existence in another world, or staying beyond what is proper for such communication to take place, is likely to degenerate into possession. When a spirit does not wish to relinquish its hold upon earth conditions, and when it continues to express such desires through the intermediary of a living person, the spiritualist considers this a case of possession. In truth, I have investigated a number of cases of which possession was claimed, which turned out to be nothing more than intense cases of communication from the next dimension. The fervor with which such communications were sought (in order to rectify past impressions left behind or to complete unfinished business) had aspects of urgency which those most closely involved mistook for possession. However, in fact it was not possession.

The spiritualistic approach involves clearly uncritical elements of belief and assumption, while at the same time utilizing factual material from the realms of parapsychology as well. Unquestionably, the spiritualist approach to possession is by far the most useful, short of the psychical research approach, because it is more likely to yield positive results than religious exorcism or purely medical treatment. In defense of religious exorcists and medical practitioners, however, it should be stated that there are individuals among them who are also aware of parapsychology and its findings and who have incorporated some of these findings into their own parochial work. They are just as likely to be successful in their endeavors as the parapsychologist may be. As with so many things, generalizations tend to be false. Not every religious exorcist is wrong, not every physician hostile to psychic evidence and, after all, not every parapsychologist successful with *his or her* method of dealing with the phenomena.

In psychic research the method employed presupposes the existence of a separate entity causing possession to take place. This entity is a human being generally no longer in the living body. Occasionally there are reports of *possession by a living person* of another. This, however, is a combination of telepathy, sometimes involves hypnosis, and always calls for an interrelationship between possessed and possessor.

The overwhelming majority of cases, however, involve possession of a living person by the spirit of a *dead* individual. For a variety of reasons the dead individual wishes to use the physical, emotional, and mental faculties of the living being for his or her own ends, regardless of the consequences and regardless of the wishes of the instrument used. However, I have found that it is *quite impossible* for possession to take place, if the individual who is possessed does not open the gates in some fashion to the possessor. Generally this is not done consciously, but it may be the result of unconscious desire or weakness which allows possession to take place.

Possession against the will of an individual with that individual fully aware of all of his or her faculties and powers and resisting possession is completely impossible. No one is taken over against his or her wishes if the person rejects such a takeover and is consciously aware of it. It is only because of some weakness in the character, or because of some overt act by the individual, that the possessor may enter. Contrary to medieval thinking and superstition, people are not possessed haphazardly, taken over unsuspectingly at odd moments. To the contrary, the act of possession is a concise invasion of the privacy of an individual by the strong and determined personality of another.

That this other individual is deceased makes the need for possession of a physical body the more urgent from his or her point of view, giving the act additional power and impetus.

We should realize that the mere act of passing from the physical state to the next dimension (where the personality continues to exist in a nonphysical world), does not render the individual angelic or in any way different from his or her state of being prior to death. Those who pass over in a state of evil or mental confusion will retain their individual ways on the other side of life. They *may* be retained by those who have gone on before them, and these confused souls may be taught the proper attitudes eventually.

Evil remains evil, whether in the body or out

of it. Since people are individuals and differ widely
in their appetites and moral standards, and since
people take their individualities with them to the
other side of life it stands to reason that among the
multitudes of discarnates populating the limitless
realms of the nonphysical world, there are many
who cannot adjust to that world and to its
standards. They long for the physical world and
the appetites associated with it, and they will do
everything in their power to return if only through
the precarious hold they may exercise upon a
living person on the earth plane. This is not a
matter of vicarious thrills experienced through the
sensory apparatus of another in possession. He or
she *is* the other person and experiences these
sensations *directly* or *intimately*.

In possession, the possessing personality
enters the physical body of the victim through one
of the solar plexuses, that is, the psychic "opening
gates" located at the top of the head and in the
stomach region. As the possessor gains hold of
nerve ganglia at these points, the entity then
connects with the nervous sytem of the individual
and merges its own personality fields with the
electromagnetic personality field of the host
personality. If the merger is complete, the host's
personality may be entirely displaced by the
possessor's own personality. In the majority of
possessions, this merger is less than complete. As
a result, there are fluctuations in the impact of the
possessing entity. At times the merger is complete, and the possessor speaks as him or herself.
At other times, the host personality is again in

control and returns to his or her normal self. Why these fluctuations occur and what controls them we do know from the multiple of cases investigated by respected scientific investigators. Having entered the nervous system of the host's body and merged the electromagnetic field of the possessor with that of the host, the possessing entity then learns to manipulate the physical apparatus of the body in which he or she has taken up residence. This takes some time, for the possessor must adjust to the individual quirks of that particular host's body. Therefore, possession is a gradual process, and it generally takes a number of days or weeks until the state of possession is seemingly complete.

With the merger of the two personality fields comes the infusion of the possessing entity's own recollections and mind into that of the host. This is somewhat like a record player onto which a new record has been placed. The player itself has no knowledge of the contents of the record but mouths it faithfully once the needle has been placed upon the record. In possession, the host personality becomes the obedient and subservient executor of the possessing entity's desires. Since it cannot anticipate these desires, the host personality is unable to do anything about it or to rid him or herself of the possessive entity without outside help.

The reasons for possession may vary greatly according to the individual character of the spirits possessing. They may be merely desirous to continue a physical type of life through another individual, or it may be due to recognition that some particular individual is especially suited to continue the needs and unfinished business of the deceased individual. In some cases the living person appeals to the power instinct of the discarnate. Often, the possessor fancies himself or herself in the notion of playing Svengali to some meek Trilby on the earth plane, enjoying the power play as an antidote to the boredom encountered on the spiritual level. This occurs because the discarnate has not yet understood the attractions and possibilities at that level and continues to regard everything from the physical point of view alone.

Eventually the possessive entity familiarizes him or herself with the thought processes and circumstances of the host personality for purposes of better control. The more he or she knows about the conditions likely to be encountered inside the body and mind of the host personality, the more likely that the possessor will be able to deal with such conditions. To defend one's hold upon the host personality is foremost in the possessor's mind. To be ejected from the host personality is what the possessor fears and fights at all costs, even sacrificing *the life* of the host to resist ejection.

The purely parapsychological approach to the problem takes into account *both* the powers of the possessing entity and the personality quirks of the victim, which made it possible for possession to take place. After research has established that it is indeed a case of possession, it is important to look for ordinary psychic communications and of course eliminate any nonpsychic possibilities, such as true mental illness, split personality, and any other rational, reasonable explanation for the phenomena one investigates. If there remains a residue of evidence pointing in the direction of true possession, then the trained parapsychologist will deal with it on two levels. He or she will accept a secondary personality as a true individual personality and deal with it directly through the person of the victim. He or she will also occupy him or herself with the exploration of the victim's own makeup to determine where the weakness lies that makes the possession possible. In directing his or her efforts simultaneously in both directions, he or she will be able to loosen the stronghold of the possessing entity over the victim and thus solve the case.

Willingness to be possessed is by no means as farfetched as it may sound. To a large number of people, the idea of having a superior will superimposed on their own will is not only acceptable but desirable. It eliminates the need for their own decisions, shifts the burden of failure from the self to the person of another, and, in general, creates a kind of dependency, which to some is a comfortable refuge from the pressures of the environment. Passive willingness to accept dominance by another is *always* present in cases of possession. In the majority of situations the victim is not even aware of it, but it is neverthless part of the syndrome. At the very least, fear of the superior influence of the possession entity, and conviction that nothing can be done about it are present in all such cases.

When the willingness or the desire to be possessed turns from passive acceptance to *active search* and initiation of the relationship, we speak of *obsession*. As the word indicates, it comes from the Latin *obsedere,* meaning "preoccupied with." The action stems from the so-called victim, not from an outside personality imposed upon the victim. In the *broadest* sense, obsession means "an abnormal desire with any subject matter" beyond the ordinary. To be obsessed with an idea refers to the inability of the individual to let go of that idea, regardless of difficulties. In common language, obsession relates to strong personal objectives, generally of emotional connotations, and it can be applied both to persons and to inanimate objects or to general subjects. Obsession is the dark twin of possession. While it is true that the *possessed* must offer some sort of collaboration to the possessor, the *obsessed* person does all the beckoning. In the narrow sense of this parapsychological term, obsession means the initiation by an individual of a relationship with a discarnate personality in which the dominance of the discarnate over the incarnate is sought out and desired. There are extremely rare cases in which obsession occurs between two living people. But it is my feeling that such cases are more properly classified as telepathic dominance, hypnosis, and, in extreme instances, mental and emotional aberration. By and large people are obsessed with the dead, not the living.

John X. is a musician. He has an average

talent and a good job with an orchestra. He wishes he could do more than he is doing, accomplish something outstanding. Accidentally, he discovers an affinity for a certain composer, long dead. He involves himself in the study of the composer's style until he becomes *obsessed* with the idea of carrying out the dead composer's work. Eventually his striving and psychic emanations reach out to the dead composer's personality and a contact is established. Now the discarnate begins to use the living musician as his instrument and obsession takes place. The living musician no longer regards his own personality as important. He lives only for the dead composer and to carry out the composer's work through his own instrumentality.

Mary Y. is engaged to be married to a young man of her acquaintance. After a few short weeks the young man is killed in a street accident. Shortly after the funeral Mary received spirit communication from the deceased. Thus far, the relationship is entirely within the realm of possibility, as seen by the open-minded psychic researcher. After a while Mary becomes convinced that she cannot ever forget her dead fiancé nor find another to take his place. To the psychologist this is a simple matter. Mary's mind is becoming unhinged due to excessive grief and her inability to adjust to the environment. But from the parapsychological point of view, something else may be happening. When an occasional communication from the deceased, generally through the mediumship of some local clairvoyant or similar person, is no longer sufficient for Mary and her entire life becomes oriented towards a resumption of the relationship with her dead fiancé, she reaches out to him in the hope of re-establishing a link. At this moment obsession takes place. In Mary's case this obsession may lead to suicide in the hope of joining her loved one on the other side of life. That this is a fallacy can be seen in the light of evidence that suicides rarely reach their goal on the other side of life, but are, to the contrary, sent "back to school", as it were, to make up that which they tried to escape on earth.

Since Mary does not commit suicide and since she cannot be on the same level as her fiancé, she becomes obsessed with him and their further love tie. The continuing relationship develops between two unequal partners, one of the flesh and one in spirit. As a result of this, Mary shuns all physical relationships on the earth plane, devoting herself entirely to her spirit lover.

The two cases I have described here are typical examples of true obsession. They are not actual cases, but are presented here as examples for obsession so that the reader may understand the basic nature of this phenomenon.

Although obession is initiated by the living person and can in theory at least be terminated by the living person, it is rare that such occurs. Unfortunately, the majority of the obsessed are incapable of rationalizing their relationship. To them, the relationship is perfectly natural and superior to ordinary situations they may encounter in their own environment. Quite rightly so. Obsessive relationships are extremely exciting and sophisticated in their own way, whereas in the majority of cases the day-to-day existence of the obsessed is anything but exciting, especially after the subject of the individual's obsession is no longer within reach. But obsession is just as destructive as possession and cannot be tolerated as a state of being for any length of time without *destroying the individual concerned*.

In the case of obsession, the religious approach has little to offer since the initiative comes from the *living person*. At the very best, *moral* issues are involved, especially when one of the partners of the obsession relationship is deceased. The medical fraternity deals with obsession with greater frequency. When obsession borders on the state of mental imbalance, a psychiatrist should treat the case as an aberration of the mind or emotional apparatus of the individual involved.

But if the underlying factors are basically healthy ones and obsession is due only to a desire on the part of the obsessed to maintain a relationship in which *something of value* can be brought from the nonphysical world into the physical world, then the approach used in parapsychology is best. Once it is established that the obsessed person is not mentally deficient, but to the contrary, in full control of his or her mental faculties (or was so prior to the onset of the obsession), the parapsychological approach may yield better results by dealing again with *both the obsessed and the contact on the other side of life separately and yet jointly.* The one who is being exorcised then is not the spirit but the flesh-and-blood personality. Or, to put it into the vernacular, the spirit is not removed from the body of the victim, but the willing victim is turned away from the spirit he or she has called up on his or her own.

Sometimes obsession turns into possession when the initiator of the process loses control and the possessive entity, originally called up by the obsessed, takes over entirely even after the obsessed desires discontinuance of the relationship. This happens particularly when someone unfamiliar with the dangers of attempted obsession or who does not take the process seriously enough, toys with it, and then, realizing the involvement, tries to withdraw but cannot do so.

On occasion, possession or even obsession has resulted from indiscriminate use of psychic materials such as Ouija boards and table-tipping devices. It is always unwise for a person *who is a potential trance medium* to open the gate to possible possession. Unfortunately there are a large number of people unaware of their own mediumship. In such cases the takeover process is unexpected and the more frightening, since the technique and resulting problems are not immediately known to the one most directly involved.

On the following pages you will find listed, with their current prices, some of the books now available on related subjects. Your book dealer stocks most of these and will stock new titles in the Llewellyn series as they become available. We urge your patronage.

TO GET A FREE CATALOG

To obtain our full catalog, you are invited to write (see address below) for our bi-monthly news magazine/catalog, *Llewellyn's New Worlds of Mind and Spirit*. A sample copy is free, and it will continue coming to you at no cost as long as you are an active mail customer. Or you may subscribe for just $10 in the United States and Canada ($20 overseas, first class mail). Many bookstores also have *New Worlds* available to their customers. Ask for it.

TO ORDER BOOKS AND TAPES

If your book store does not carry the titles described on the following pages, you may order them directly from Llewellyn by sending the full price in U.S. funds, plus postage and handling (see below).

Credit card orders: VISA, MasterCard, American Express are accepted. Call us toll-free within the United States and Canada at 1-800-THE-MOON.

Postage and Handling: Include $4 postage and handling for orders $15 and under; $5 for orders *over* $15. There are no postage and handling charges for orders over $100. Postage and handling rates are subject to change. We ship UPS whenever possible within the continental United States; delivery is guaranteed. Please provide your street address as UPS does not deliver to P.O. boxes. Orders shipped to Alaska, Hawaii, Canada, Mexico and Puerto Rico will be sent via first class mail. Allow 4-6 weeks for delivery. **International orders:** Airmail – add retail price of each book and $5 for each non-book item (audiotapes, etc.); Surface mail – add $1 per item.

Minnesota residents please add 7% sales tax.

Llewellyn Worldwide
P.O. Box 64383-367, St. Paul, MN 55164-0383, U.S.A.

For customer service, call (612) 291-1970.

Prices subject to change without notice.

ESP, WITCHES & UFOS:
The Best of Hans Holzer, Book II
Edited by Ray Buckland

In this exciting anthology, best-selling author and psychic investigator Hans Holzer explores true accounts of the strange and unknown: telepathy, psychic and reincarnation dreams, survival after death, psycho-ecstasy, unorthodox healings, Pagans and Witches, and Ufonauts. Reports included in this volume:

• Mrs. F. dreamed of a group of killers and was particularly frightened by the eyes of their leader. Ten days later, the Sharon Tate murders broke into the headlines. When Mrs. F. saw the photo of Charles Manson, she immediately recognized him as the man from her dream.

• How you can use four simple "wish-fulfillment" steps to achieve psycho-ecstasy—turning a negative situation into something positive.

• Several true accounts of miraculous healings achieved by unorthodox medical practitioners.

• How the author, when late to meet with a friend and unable to find a telephone nearby, sent a telepathic message to his friend via his friend's answering service.

• The reasons why more and more people are turning to Witchcraft and Paganism as a way of life.

• When UFOs land—physical evidence vs. cultists.

These reports and many more will entertain and enlighten all readers intrigued by the mysteries of life … and beyond!

0-87542-368-X, 304 pgs., mass market $4.95

EXTRA-TERRESTRIALS AMONG US
by George C. Andrews

According to the law, if the government wishes to enforce it, anyone found guilty of E.T. contact is to be quarantined indefinitely under armed guard. Does that sound like the government doesn't take Extra-Terrestrials seriously? This book exposes the government's cover-up about UFOs and their occupants, setting the stage for a "Cosmic Watergate."

Author George Andrews researched the evidence concerning E.T. intervention in human affairs for more than a decade before presenting his startling conclusions. *Extra-Terrestrials Among Us* is an exciting challenge to "orthodox" thinking which presents fascinating, documented case histories of cattle mutilations, lights in the sky, circular flying machines, strange disappearances, objects falling from the sky and spontaneous combustion. Here also is the story of CIA involvement, Nazi contacts, Martian landings, and much more. If you believe in E.T.s, or if you're not really sure, *Extra-Terrestrials Among Us* will open you eyes to new worlds.

0-87542-001-X, 304 pgs., mass market, illus., photos $4.95

DOORS TO OTHER WORLDS
A Practical Guide to Communicating with Spirits
by Raymond Buckland

A recent revival of spiritualism has more people attempting to communicate with disembodied spirits via talking boards, séances, and all forms of mediumship—allowing another spirit to make use of your vocal chords, hand muscles, etc., while you remain in control of your body. The movement, which began in 1848 with the Fox sisters of New York, has attracted the likes of Abraham Lincoln and Queen Victoria, and even blossomed into a full-scale religion with regular services of hymns, prayers, Bible-reading and sermons along with spirit communication.

Explore the nature of the Spiritual Body, learn how to prepare yourself to become a medium, experience for yourself the trance state, clairvoyance, psychometry, table tipping and levitation, talking boards, automatic writing, spiritual photography, spiritual healing, distant healing, channeling, development circles, and also learn how to avoid spiritual fraud.

0-87542-061-3, 272 pgs., 5 ¼x 8, illus., softcover $10.00

A PRACTICAL GUIDE TO PAST LIFE REGRESSION
by Florence Wagner McClain

Have you ever felt that there had to be more to life than this? Have you ever met someone and felt an immediate kinship? Have you ever visited a strange place and felt that you had been there before? Have you struggled with frustrations and fears which seem to have no basis in your present life? Are you afraid of death? Have you ever been curious about reincarnation or maybe just interested enough to be skeptical?

This book presents a simple technique which you can use to obtain past life information TODAY. There are no mysterious preparations, no groups to join, no philosophy to which you must adhere. You don't even have to believe in reincarnation. The tools are provided for you to make your own investigations, find your own answers and make your own judgements as to the validity of the information and its usefulness to you.

Whether or not you believe in reincarnation, past life regression remains a powerful and valid tool for self-exploration. Information procured through this procedure can be invaluable for personal growth and inner healing, no matter what its source. Florence McClain's guidebook is an eminently sane and capable guide for those who wish to explore their possible past lives or conduct regressions themselves.

0-87542-510-0, 160 pgs., 5¼ x 8, softcover $7.95